CANTERBURY

Series edited by Dennis Sharp

Frontispiece: The nave of Canterbury Cathedral
looking south-east from the north aisle.
Engraving from *Cathedral Antiquities: Canterbury Cathedral Church*, published by Longman
& Company, 1822.

CANTERBURY

Sherban Cantacuzino

Hamish Halls

Flavia Petrie

David Woodcock

with an introduction by

Robert Paine

Studio Vista

*Produced by November Books Limited,
23–9 Emerald Street, London, WC1N 3QL.*

*Published by Studio Vista Limited, Blue Star
House, Highgate Hill, London, N19.*

*Text set by Yendall & Company Limited,
Riscatype House, 22–5 Red Lion Court, Fleet
Street, London, EC4.*

*Printed by Compton Printing Limited, Pembroke
Road, Stocklake, Aylesbury, Bucks.*

*Bound by Dorstel Press Limited, West Road,
Templefields, Harlow, Essex.*

SBN 289.79802.7

*Acknowledgments for photographs and other
illustrations*

Architectural Press: 129; Peter Baistow: 122;
Patrick Browne: 54, 75A, 90; Bernard Cadd:
117; Sherban Cantacuzino: 1, 4, 5A, 7, 8, 10,
11, 13, 14, 15, 16, 17, 19, 20, 21, 22, 24, 25, 26,
27, 28, 29, 30, 31, 32, 33, 34, 35, 36, 37, 40, 41,
43, 44, 45, 46, 47, 48, 49, 51A, 52, 56, 58, 60,
63, 64, 65, 66, 67, 68, 69, 70, 71, 72, 73, 75B,
76A, 77, 78, 79, 80, 81, 82, 83, 84A, 84B, 87,
88, 89, 91, 92, 93, 94, 95, 97, 98, 99, 101, 102,
103, 106, 114, 121A; City of Canterbury: 104;
John Clague: 125; Entwhistle Photographic
Services: 3, 5B, 9, 18, 38, 39, 42, 59, 74, 76B,
96, 110, 112, 120; Hamish Halls: 2, 12, 23;
Sam Lambert: 128; Anthony Mauduit: 121B;
National Monuments Record: 55; Robert
Paine and Partners: 131; Henk Snoek: 126;
William Toomey: 86; University of Kent at
Canterbury: 116, 131; David Woodcock: 50,
51B, 53, 57, 61, 62, 105, 107, 108, 109, 111,
113A, 113B, 115, 118, 119, 123, 124, 127.

ACKNOWLEDGMENTS

he compilation of a work of this kind depends eavily on published material and the authors ish to offer special thanks to Mr Frank iggenbottam, Librarian, and to the staff of ie Canterbury Public Library; to Canon obinson, Canon Librarian, and to the staff of ie Cathedral Library; and to the staff of the IBA Library, London. They also wish to ank Mr John Newman for permission to see ie proofs of 'Kent' in the *Buildings of England* ries to be published shortly by Penguin; Mr hn Piper for making available proofs of ennethorne Hughes' 'Shell Guide of Kent' nce published by Faber; and in addition to r William Urry, Reverend D. Ingram-Hill, nd Mr Patrick Brown, who made their own ublications available and also gave us the enefit of their great knowledge of the city.

Valuable information and assistance has also een given by

The Dean of Canterbury

City of Canterbury Architect's, Education, Engineer and Surveyor's, Housing, and Town Clerk's Departments

Kent County Council, Architect's Department

Management of Westminster Bank Limited nd by

Mr D. F. Andrews, Secretary of the Kent and Canterbury Club

Mr Bernard Cadd, William Holford and Partners, Architects

Dr and Mrs P. Cassidi

Mr John C. Clague, Architect

Mr W. C. Day, Vice Principal, Canterbury College of Art

Mr David Edwards, Surveyor and Deputy Registrar, University of Kent

Mr S. Gaddesden, Building Inspector, for searching in old records

Mrs W. M. Head

Canon C. H. de Laubenque, Roman Catholic Church of St Thomas Becket

Rev R. H. Mansfield-Williams, Vicar of St Gregory-the-Great

Mr Peter Marsh, Dudley Marsh, Son and Partner, Architects

Mr Anthony Mauduit, Architect

Mr W. R. Mowll and Mr J. E. S. Brick of Mowll and Mowll, Solicitors

Messrs Nasons of Canterbury

Messrs Robert Paine and Partners, Architects

Mr E. W. Parkin

Mr J. W. Pope, Director, Lefevre's Ltd

Mr Brian Raffety of Kingsford, Arrowsmith and Wightwick, Solicitors

Mr David Riceman, Director, Riceman's of Canterbury

Mr Anthony Swaine, Architect

Mr H. A. Turner, Assistant Secretary, Canterbury Group Hospital Management Committee

Mr Francis Voigt, King's School

Mr H. W. Warner

Miss Warters of the Clergy Orphan Corporation

Mr and Mrs Stephen Williamson

Mr B. W. J. G. Wilson, King's School

Miss I. V. Young, Deputy Principal, Christ Church College

and by many others who allowed access to their buildings.

Help with research and drawing has been given by Miss Tessa Browne, Miss Jenny Cousins, Mr Paul Gummer, Miss Mary Rosseter, and Miss Julienne Winfield; and permission to use their measured drawings of the Church of St Dunstan by Mr G. E. Smith and of the Warehouses, Pound Lane, by Mr David Watson.

NTRODUCTION

is significant that though once a city occupied y the Romans, Canterbury most decisively jected its Roman name: *Durovernum* became antwarabyrig – the place of the men of Kent. anes troubled it, Normans and Angevins left arks here and there, but with its motley collection of gabled buildings it is English. It is so very small, a city in Lewis Mumford's nse, but in miniature. Despite modern growth eyond the core, it remains a perceptible tefact, easy to comprehend and clearly articuted.

Even with the competition of recent building e great bulk of the Cathedral still dominates. Iany people may no longer subscribe to what stands for but one cannot ignore the order e building imposes on Canterbury. Nowhere an this be better seen than from the top of Bell Iarry, below which is spread out a rich xture of orange-brown roofs, sometimes as any as six pitches to a single building, all n the same module. Visitors come in their iousands every year intending only to look t the Cathedral, but stay to absorb the city. anterbury's universality is apparent.

Ironically, the fact that it is a city is the anger which threatens it most. It may, as Iayor John Twyne declared, be 'no Mean ity', but it no longer comprises what this vord has come to signify. Planning appropriate Birmingham or even York is quite unsuited ere. In Buchanan terms, the central area is no nore than a single precinct, yet traffic threatens : with death by congestion.

The city has a curious form. A cell roughly void within its wall, or the line where the wall nce ran, it has adhering to it on the inner side sub-cell (the Precinct of Christ Church) vhich contained one of two generative forces – eligion. Clinging to it on the outside are the emains of the second great religious enclave, it Augustine's. Trade, the other generator, ontrived to occupy most of the remaining pace within the wall line, following a pattern ather as if the Roman layout had been dropped nd put together again by one who only half inderstood it. Add that this pattern accepts the lominance of a development around the wall nd another around the Precinct's inner line, nd the whole has a rich variety and excitement. n this is yet another element of Englishness vhich creates the city's appeal; it provokes motional reactions rather than intellectual reflections.

If on the whole Canterbury prompts response first from the heart, inspiring a love which transcends the irritation of its parochialism, it contains in the Cathedral one of the truly great works of intellect applied to architecture. Henry Yevele's nave is the quintessence of great architecture, intellectual but free of arrogance, totally without theatricality, an anticipation of that modulated poise which once carried the English ideal round the world. Built in the 14th century, the nave also stands as a witness to the skill and mastery of its masons, its roof carpenters and its glaziers.

Complementary to the Cathedral and a prelude to it, Mercery Lane and the Buttermarket, in form like a pan-handle to the chafing dish of the Precinct, reveal these same craftsmen at work unaided. Masters of timber-framed construction, they met the challenge of demand posed by the great pilgrimages with a superb array of tight packed hostelries. Adapted and re-adapted, those which survived senseless destruction or disaster stand in close order, jettied across the narrow lane or clustered round the market. Aimed towards Christ Church gate and framing it in a vista, the lane and the tiny market are full always of a play of light and shade.

The basic materials of Canterbury are few and simple; timber eked out with brick, tiles (as well as tiles which simulate bricks) and a great deal of flint and rubble stone bequeathed by Romans and the monastic builders, and constantly re-used. Exceptional to them is the mild Caen stone of the Cathedral which, though foreign to the remainder, harmonises completely. There is a great deal of rendering and painting, fortunately much still in the old blacks and whites and reds and browns, all enriching the diversity of small-scale pattern.

As an urban environment Canterbury has all the virtues which have been preached about from Vitruvius to Gordon Cullen. In it there is no conflict between theoretical concepts and human needs. It is the direct response to climate, and to circumstance which come easily to people who live with nature. Until recently it was untouched by casuistical sophistication. Today it is still basically a mediæval city, not much modified within its walls by the activities of later generations; it has shown great capacity to absorb their works without any diminishing of its distinctive character. This is particularly evident in the main street where the most recent buildings consort with neo-Georgian, with Victorian, art nouveau and Edwardian, all absorbed into the higgledy-piggledy of timber frame and gable, itself often disguised by a veneer of mathematical tiles and a rustic cornice. Nowhere is this better seen than from the Post Office looking towards Yevele's massive West-gate.

Victorianism sits surprisingly well on Canterbury. Time and again the most fantastic of its nonsense was absorbed successfully into an already rich mix. At its best, as in Butterfield's work at St Augustine's and Hardwick's St Edmunds on St Thomas's Hill, it gave weight to the otherwise generally domestic.

Fortunately Canterbury escaped the fate of other blitzed cities like Exeter and Coventry, and fell prey neither to the brave-new-world men nor to the 'high-class' developers. Hugh Wilson's post-war plan has been much criticised for some aspects which time has shown he might himself have modified. What was executed of it in his day was conceived while he was still that romantic self which created the best of early Cumbernauld when planning was for people and Camillo Sitte the planners' hero. Luckily what threatened thereafter to be an epidemic of curtain wall and tinted panel was halted by a cold wind from Whitehall. Now chance, which has played much part in Canterbury's history, seems intent to intervene again. The University is creeping in from behind bringing with it a zest, fashionable perhaps, for town life and urban dwelling. Areas for long blighted are coming to life. Given that the cars can be moved out or tidied away, the city may for the first time in its long history become fully built up; it was never so in Roman times, nor afterwards. This way, too, it may become the first to show that a city by night, properly inhabited, need not be like a tomb.

In such development the pedestrian is the clue. Pedestrian scale is vital not merely for safety and comfort, but in this case because the city is so small. Open it to traffic and the illusion of size, of the more-beyond, vanishes. It becomes an incident on a highway. Loitering with no intent whatsoever is what people seek in towns, not windy walkways nor island hops in traffic streams. The Precincts and the King's School – Oxford in miniature – what is left of the old town, the new core contrived by Hugh Wilson and John Berbiers, and parts of St Dunstan's yield these delights.

Less so the University which, had it occupied the old military area, would have added a new dimension, a whole new quarter to the City. That public money spent so lavishly should yield some benefits to existing environment would be reasonable to expect. Instead the University stands widespread and in windy isolation on the northern horizon, providing much athletic exercise and, for future architectural historians, a study in mid-century mannerism. East and west, the built-up area spreads now to the very limit of the rural boundary. New quarters fill with housing, some quite pleasing, but not particularly identifiable with Canterbury more than any other place. To the south a great hospital complex is developing fast. But it is to the centre that the mind returns where the still considerable task of filling the vacancies of war challenges the essence of the old city. What constitutes that essence can be felt by all who are prepared to seek it out on foot. Canterbury took shape in a non-materialist age, and now, when the materialist society is being challenged, to preserve Canterbury as a symbol and inspiration must be the concern of everyone.

Robert Paine

Canterbury, January 1970

City Architects of Canterbury

Hugh Wilson 1945–56
John Berbiers 1957–65
Donald Tomkinson 1966–

Bibliography

John Newman, *Buildings of England – Kent, Vol. 1*. Harmondsworth, Penguin Books, 1970.

Pennethorne Hughes, *A Shell Guide*. London, Faber, 1969.

William Townsend, *Canterbury*. London, Batsford, 1950.

Herbert Waddams, *The Pictorial History of Canterbury*. Pitkin Pictorials, 1968.

Richard Church, *Portrait of Canterbury*. London, Hutchinson, 1968.

D. Ingram Hill, *The Ancient Hospitals and Almshouses of Canterbury*. Canterbury Archæological Society, 1969.

W. Urry, *Canterbury under the Angevin Kings*. London, Athlone Press, 1967.

E. Hasted, *History of Canterbury*. Simmons and Kirkby, 1774, 1777, 1795, 1805; W. Blackley, 1825.

One of the best ways of following the development of a town is by studying old maps, and the following are available on request in the reference library of the Beaney Institute, High Street, Canterbury: Speed (1611), William and Henry Doidge (1752), Andrews and Wren (1768), Gostling (1774) and subsequent editions, Mudge's first Ordnance Survey (1801 and subsequent revisions), Vernor, Hood and Sharpe (1806), and Longman's (publishers, 1822).

GAZETTEER

1

PARISH CHURCH OF ST MARTIN
St Martin's Hill   **A.D. 600 and later**

The oldest parish church in England, it has been in continuous use for 14 centuries, and provides a fitting, even if rather daunting, introduction to Canterbury's multifarious architectural styles. The church is of profound historical and architectural interest. It was here, according to Bede, that a disused Roman church lying to the east of the city was given to Bertha, Ethelbert's Christian queen, as a place of worship in 562. Here also it was that St Augustine and his companions first met and worshipped in c. 597 before the first new churches were built; and in all probability that Ethelbert himself was baptised.

Although a great deal of the structure consists of Roman tiles laid with some knowledge of Roman methods, none of the original Roman walling is now considered to remain as it origi-

nally stood. The western part of the chancel ◀◀
seems to be all that exists from the earliest phase 1
of Anglo-Saxon work of c. 600–50, and is presumably an example of the rebuilding that King Ethelbert permitted Augustine to carry out. On the south side, at the extreme west end of the chancel, is a blocked door with a straight stone lintel that originally led into a *porticus*. A round-headed doorway (now blocked) was let into the wall just east of this, slightly later but still before 650. The chancel was extended in the 13th century and lancets were inserted in the 7th-century walls. The nave, like the round-headed door, was added later in the first half of the 7th century. The walls lack the regularity of true Roman work and are strengthened by characteristic early Saxon thin buttresses. The nave too has been much remodelled in later centuries. The flint tower is 14th century, but uses early masonry and Roman bricks.

What is revealed of the masonry within tells the same story. In the north wall of the western chancel is a recessed tomb, once thought to be the burial place of Queen Bertha. The west wall of the nave provides a separate puzzle. The unplastered wall shows the outline of what may have been a lofty west doorway, or door surmounted by a window, and flanked by a pair of blocked, round-headed windows that have themselves been reworked and modified within the Anglo-Saxon period. Also within the nave is the controversial font. Unusually it is made of some score of stone blocks, and has traditionally been claimed as the font in which King Ethelbert was baptised. The intersecting arcade below the rim and the use of beading on the arches and intersecting rings inform the whole with a Norman Romanesque flavour; but the arches and beads could have been added later to an originally smaller font decorated with plain intersecting strapwork rings. But why is it made of Caen stone? Was Caen stone known before it was introduced under Norman influence? One is tempted to call it 'Anglo-Saxon Romanesque', which conveniently dissociates it from King Ethelbert and William the Conqueror alike.

2

CHURCH OF ST NICOLAS
Harbledown   **11th Century and later**

Between 1085 and 1096 Lanfranc, the first Norman archbishop, founded St Nicolas as a hospital for lepers. It is entered through a wooden gatehouse, but the present hospital buildings date from 1840 and are still used as almshouses

(though no longer, of course, for lepers). The adjoining church consists of nave and aisles all under one great roof. Much Norman work survives: the tower and the west door of the nave with its outer chevron moulding, several small round-headed windows, and herring-bone masonry with a few Roman bricks in the west wall. The church was remodelled in the Decorated and Perpendicular Gothic periods. The Decorated window at the east end of the north aisle has a hood mould with label stops carved as heads wrapped in wimples. Despite the Gothic remodelling the interior is refreshingly unrestored and uncluttered Norman. The earlier north arcade of round arches has well preserved carved ornamentation. The south arcade is late 12th century, being essentially Romanesque in spirit though pointed. In the chancel are some 13th-century stalls and frescoes of saints in the east window splays.

3
HOSPITAL OF ST THOMAS THE MARTYR UPON EASTBRIDGE
The King's Bridge   **12th Century and later**
This hospice for poor pilgrims was founded before 1180 and much of the work of this period remains: the refectory and the remarkable undercroft below. One enters through a Gothic doorway set below a larger 12th-century arch in the unremarkable flint façade. One is now in a 2-bay vestibule covered by one ribbed and one groin vault. To the left is another vaulted chamber, now a chapel, and straight ahead down more steps is the undercroft. Four small columns support a groin-vaulted hall, still essentially Romanesque in character, in which the

pilgrims slept. A small compartment off the south-west corner overlooks the Stour. Above this room is the refectory hall. It is also of the late 12th century, with a wonderfully preserved fresco (early 13th century) depicting Christ in Majesty surrounded by smaller representations of the four Evangelists with their appropriate symbols. One immediately thinks of the Majesty at Berzé la Ville, though there are marked stylistic and iconographical differences between the two. The pointed 3-arched arcade here is more aware of the new Gothic style, and the capitals surmounting the octagonal piers are a flattened form of crocket.

Up the next flight of stairs is the chapel, which dates from *c.* 1363 when the present 2-storey façade was built. It is lit by three Perpendicular windows; like the refectory it has a crown post roof (typical of Canterbury) and also an unusual bell cage of oak. About 1584 the hostel was converted into an almshouse, the brothers occupying the wing over the Stour itself, which was brick-faced in 1660–3. At the time of writing, the hospital is about to be modernised so as to continue its work as an almshouse.

4
CASTLE   **12th Century**
Castle Street
The quadrangular shell of the Great Keep is the remains of one of many castles constructed by the Normans. The present ruins are of a fortification completed in 1174. The platform is of rubble and Roman brick, but the walls themselves are of a more orderly construction of stone repaired with flint. The interiors of the

3 ◄

4 ◄

walls are faced with flint. Loop-holes pierce the walls here and there. Henry Yevele, who also worked on the Cathedral and probably the West-gate (21), was responsible for renovations be-tween 1378 and 1385, and some of the finely squared masonry on the remains of the corner towers must be attributed to him. Since 1597 the castle has decayed under private ownership. In 1817 the upper story was demolished, leav-ing the wall passage open to the sky. This can be reached by the spiral staircase in the eastern-most corner. Until 1928 the keep was used as a coal store, but at the time of writing it is being maintained.

5
CATHEDRAL CHURCH OF CHRIST
12th Century and later
Evidence remains of the work of many periods, but the Cathedral as it now stands is a result

essentially of three main building campaigns: (i) the second phase of Norman work (1107–30) under the Priors Ernulf and Conrad, at the time of Archbishop Anselm, which consists mainly of the western part of the crypt and a large part of the exterior of the choir and eastern transept; (ii) the early Gothic 'new' choir designed by William of Sens after the fire of 1174; (iii) the Perpendicular nave designed by Henry Yevele in c. 1380 and finally capped by Bell Harry tower begun c. 1490 by John Wastell.

Crypt: entering the crypt from the nave's magnificence one is apt to forget that this is the finest and grandest Romanesque crypt in England. Allowing for a few additions, this is the crypt as Becket knew it, and from it we can mentally reconstruct the plan of Conrad's choir above. The nave is apsidal and nine bays long by three bays wide (not counting the side aisles). It is separated from the aisles by massive piers supporting the choir above. The aisles continue round the apse to form an ambulatory, now encumbered by two hefty columns introduced by English William (William of Sens' successor) to support the new Gothic choir. From here a narrow opening leads into the eastern crypt, seldom visited, but a fine and unadorned early Gothic undercroft.

The nave of the western crypt is supported by sixteen small Norman columns, the shafts of
►► many of them carved in patterns and sur-
5 mounted by capitals. Plain cushion and scalloped capitals are interspersed with others that are delightfully carved in a number of individual styles. In some cases the Norman love for abstract decoration is admirably adapted to emphasising the shape of a cushion capital (see also the Chapel of the Holy Innocents to the north); in others the sculptors have used amusing figurative representations of everyday scenes (e.g. a pair of jongleurs) or such animals as a proud, heraldic lion or a two-headed monster. One of the most famous of these capitals is in the Chapel of St Gabriel (to the south, usually locked owing to the delicate state of 12th-century wall paintings within) where there are fabulous scenes of animals playing musical instruments, inspired by similar subjects used in illuminated manuscripts by the Canterbury scriptorium at about this time. These carvings are the beginning of the sculptural revival for which the School of Canterbury became famous. A few of the carvings are unfinished, which suggests they were carved *in situ*. An approximate date for them would thus be 1120. (One capital, of debased Corinthian design, has clearly been re-used from Archbishop Lanfranc's earlier church and dates from c. 1075.)

Choir: the east end, viewed from the crossing, presents a curious composition, resulting from the monks' desire to preserve as much of their old choir as possible after the fire of 1174. The chapels of St Anselm and St Andrew were preserved more or less intact, but following the curve of the old ambulatory (from which they were entered) they face inwards and not due east. Thus, shortly east of the eastern transepts

the choir narrows, hesitates as the flights of steps are reached, and then opens out into the Trinity Chapel with its ambulatory, and thence into the Corona or Becket's Crown. The early Gothic style here was largely imported ready-made by William of Sens, the master mason, and shows in its twin columns in the Trinity Chapel, and its very French capitals, a direct link with the nearly contemporary Cathedral of Sens. The monks, despite their love of tradition and of their old church, readily accepted the new Continental building style (could Becket's own Norman-French ancestry have helped?); but though French in origin, the 'new' choir, especially under William the Englishman who succeeded William of Sens after the latter's fall from the scaffolding in 1178, introduces a number of motives that were to become typically English. The two pairs of transepts were retained from Conrad's plan, and this arrangement, though often used in France (notably at Cluny) was enthusiastically copied in many English Gothic plans. Many decorative features here introduced became standard English items, for instance the clusters of marble engaged shafts, the rows of rhythmically grouped lancet windows, and the horizontal emphasis of string courses within and without. One cannot leave

the choir without mentioning the splendid collection of late 12th-century and early 13th-century stained glass, unique in England and equal in quality to those of Chartres and Bourges. It is described in detail in the guide by Bernard Rackham.

Nave: if the choir represents the beginning of the Gothic style in England, the nave could be said to herald its end. Though not guilty of theatricality, it was undoubtedly designed with an eye to visual effect which leads the gaze from a preferred viewpoint at the west end towards the climax of the first flight of steps and Prior

Chillenden's screen (*c.* 1400), splendidly illuminated by the lantern of Bell Harry tower. Thus while the form remains mediæval, aesthetically the renaissance is at hand. In 1378 it was decided to renew the 300-year-old Norman nave of Lanfranc. The man chosen to design it was one of England's greatest architects of all time, Henry Yevele, whose hand, and those of his followers, can be descried in many buildings in the city (see nos. 4, 21, 22), in other parts of Kent and, of course, in London. This time the old fabric was taken down and the nave rebuilt in Caen stone, like the rest of the Cathedral. At Winchester at this time the same problem was met by remodelling and refacing the Norman nave; however, the effect at Canterbury is almost identical since the new piers were raised on the Norman foundations. Thus the plan remained unchanged. The vault, however, is very lofty, for though the nave floor is lower than that of the choir, the ridge of the vault was raised into line with the choir's to provide continuity. The aisles in proportion have an even greater effect of loftiness, giving the whole nave the general appearance of a hall church – an effect found in other churches in Canterbury.

Aesthetically this striving upwards is emphasised by the tall arcade and subtly tapering vaulting shafts rising unbroken, apart from two sets of rings, to the springing of the ribs, and supporting a majestic, but by no means overbearing, lierne vault. The clerestory is minimal and all lighting comes from Yevele's fine, but simply designed, Perpendicular aisle windows. Yevele was the foremost court mason of his day and designer of the masonry of Westminster Hall, and the effect of the nave is magnificent

and palatial. Precision and the use of repetitive panels were needed to achieve this and may result in the feeling that one is entering a cold and impersonal age by comparison with that of the markedly individual work in the crypt. Geoffrey Webb discerns a French flavour in the elegance of the nave, and this might well be expected in the generation that produced the Wilton Diptych; but the flavour is subtle by comparison with the overt and purposeful French qualities in Yevele's contemporary design for the nave of Westminster Abbey. As the greatest and most independent exponent of the leading architectural style of the late Gothic world he had no need to be consciously French at Canterbury. The south-western tower at the end of the nave was designed in *c.* 1424 by Thomas Mapilton, a follower of Yevele, and the north-western one copied it as late as the 1830s when the original Norman tower was dismantled. The crowning glory of the building is, of course, Bell Harry tower over the crossing of the western transept. It was built from *c.* 1494–1503 by John Wastell, who later put the finishing touches to King's College Chapel, Cambridge. Beneath the regal array of stone arcades and pinnacles is a core of brick (a favourite material of Tudor builders).

These three chief components of the Cathedral may appear to be in marked contrast to one another stylistically. It should, however, be borne in mind not only that the nave relates, as shown, to the choir and to Lanfranc's Norman cathedral, but that the choir, on its part, is a product of the world of St Anselm, under whose archiepiscopate the western crypt was built. For the early Gothic style, in its employment of unassailable logic and building science to house and to symbolise the Divine Mystery, is a direct parallel to the scholastic philosophy very largely begun by the application of dialectic to Christian dogma that characterises St Anselm's writing. Furthermore, Colin Dudley has suggested that the measurements of all parts of the Cathedral, nave, choir or any addition, are related directly, by means of sacred geometry, to the original dimensions of Lanfranc's building. The parts may thus be said to be related essentially but divided superficially.

6
THE KING'S SCHOOL AND CATHEDRAL PRECINCTS   12th–16th Century

North of the Cathedral lies the remainder of what was once the Priory of Christchurch. Most of the surviving buildings, though by no means all, now belong to the King's School, an ancient foundation which gives Canterbury Cathedral the right to claim a seat of learning associated with it almost continuously from the time of St Augustine.

North of the nave is the cloister. Fragments of early work remain (the Norman doorway in the east walk, an early English arcade, c. 1220, in the wall of the north walk), but the fabric is essentially that of c. 1400, probably by Stephen Lote, Henry Yevele's partner who completed the nave. The late flowering of the courtly age of chivalry covered the richly ribbed vault with several hundred heraldic bosses. In the south

walk a few grotesque bosses and green men survive, and in the east walk is a head that is claimed as a portrait of Henry Yevele himself. Off the east walk is the Chapter House of c. 1300, the upper storey having been remodelled c. 1400. Heading east from the cloister one passes the Norman water tower in the Infirmary Cloister, kernel of Prior Wibert's mid-12th-century water supply, and finally reaches the remains of the Norman Infirmary and Infirmary Chapel. Back towards the Infirmary Cloister and through the Dark Entry (noting the surviving coupled cloister columns) where the Prior's mansion stood, one comes to the Green Court, now the main quadrangle of the King's School. Building here dates from all periods, with remains of original Priory buildings appearing here and there – for instance the late Norman arches in the Archdeacon's potting shed and the late mediæval towers that adjoin the Deanery. Of special note are the charming timber pentise running from Palace Court to Chillenden's Chambers (Archdeacon's residence); the Grange, originally the granary but rebuilt in the mid-16th century (dated 1566 above door) and later, which is now used by the School, and the King's School Library. This latter building, of the mid-12th century, is supported on three arches – a motif ultimately derived from the triumphal arch. It incorporates a grand tunnel-vaulted gateway (remodelled in the late Middle Ages into two smaller gates with four-centred arches) surmounted by a guest chamber, or 'Strangers'

▶
6a

Hall', after the manner of the gatehouse at Lorsch (c. 800). The chamber was used by poorer guests and pilgrims and is reached by the Norman staircase at the north end. The round-arched windows are grouped in rhythmical triplets above each arch.

7
TOWER OF THE CHURCH OF
ST GEORGE   **12th Century and later**
St George's Street
This is all that remains of the ancient Church of St George, at the south-west corner of which

this tower stood, after the air raid of 1 June 1942. The overall form is Perpendicular as is the embattled top storey, but this tower of flints bears evidence of the early 12th-century church first documented in 1165, notably the Norman west door with its round arch and simple roll moulding.

8
THE HOSPITAL OF ST JOHN THE
BAPTIST   **12th Century and later**
Northgate
Founded in 1085 by Archbishop Lanfranc,

sists of a blocked early English arcade of three bays. A ruined Norman building lies to the north-west.

9
COGAN'S HOUSE   1200 and later
St Peter's Street

This was originally a stone house standing back from the street and built by William Cokyn as the Hospital of St Nicholas and St Catharine. The present front has gables of the late 16th century and a shop front of the late 19th century. The original entrance, a small Gothic doorway, is all that visibly remains from *c.* 1200. It is now situated indoors. The glory of the house is its hall, a large aisled room under a lofty cross-braced timber roof, whose structure probably dates from the late 14th century. A partition wall now divides the hall, which no longer rises the full height of the house. The walls are covered with panelling of superb craftsmanship of *c.* 1520. Here also are two wooden corbels, once on the front of the house, depicting a dragon and the Pelican in her Piety. John Cogan, who lived here in the mid-17th century, bequeathed his house as a hospital for six clergymen's widows, and thus it remained until 1870. The house is now a private residence [see also (90)].

10
TUDOR HOUSE   1250 and later
8, Palace Street

The remains of the original stone house of the parish priest of St Alphege (*c.* 1250) can be seen on the ground floor, which is now an antique shop. (The rest of the premises is a private residence.) A central pier and arches support joists which in turn hold the flags of the stone floor above. Lancets and early English doorways also remain. About 1495 the front was modernised with a timber frame and jettied first floor, and in the first half of the 17th century a second floor was added to give the present double overhang form. The picturesque

these are perhaps the oldest almshouses still in use. In the half-timbered gate house much late mediæval wood still remains, but the other buildings were greatly restored in the mid-19th century. Though the fabric of the chapel is almost entirely 19th-century, the restoration clearly imitated a simply decorated Norman doorway at the west end and two early English lancets in the south side. The north wall con-

9a

9b

appearance is enhanced by the carved bressumers and brackets – harpies above the door and demons supporting the second floor.

11
GREYFRIARS' HOUSE   c. 1267
Off Stour Street

In 1224 the Franciscans first came to Canterbury and this is the only remaining building of the first friary they built in England. It was begun c. 1267 when the Friars were granted the land and consists of an undercroft with dormitory and warden's room above. It is built of stone and flint across a branch of the Stour, and is supported at either end by a round pillar and two 13th-century arches. All these early details are simple and utilitarian and are typical of all friars' building at this time, but c. 1450 part of the roof was raised, a fireplace inserted and the walls reinforced with narrow bricks. From c. 1482 the Friary became one of the six houses of Friars Observants in England – an ascetic order aimed at reforming contemporary laxity. They did not, however, remove the fireplace. It is said that the poet Lovelace lived here, probably in the years of poverty at the end of his life (c. 1650). After the dissolution of the monasteries (1538) the building was much altered, but was carefully restored to some likeness of the original in 1919.

12
PARISH CHURCH OF ST ALPHEGE
13th and 15th Centuries
Corner of Palace Street and St Alphege Lane
A 2-aisled hall church of flint dedicated to the first archbishop to suffer a violent death. The aisles

are of equal height and nearly equal bread [cf. St Mildred's (29) and the original form St Paul's (13)], and both show evidence of th major reconstruction of c. 1250 (blocked ea lancets in nave, lancet window – perhaps res – in the north wall, and arch into tower). Th crocketed archway of the rood loft stairs is a that remains of a screen that spanned bot aisles. The remodelled Perpendicular windov and arcade date from c. 1495, the piers seemin to follow the style developed at St Mildred' The interior has the atmosphere of a villa, church, and this is typical of Canterbury – city whose churches seem to have left the cult vation of urbanity to the cathedral, and who parishes still maintain individual and distin characters.

13
PARISH CHURCH OF ST PAUL
Church Street St Paul's   13th Centu

Originally this was another of Canterbury's aisled hall churches, of the 13th century, as shown by the arches from the tower into th nave and north aisle, and by the north arcad But in 1856 it was almost completely rebuilt b Sir Gilbert Scott on a similar plan to St Marg ret's (17), which he had restored about six yea before, to become a 3-aisled hall church. Sco added the south arcade (a copy of the north on and south aisle, the eastern part of the nort wall, restored the upper storey of the tower wi its pyramidal roof, and fitted his favour Decorated (or 'middle pointed') windov throughout. The centre aisle (previously ju the south aisle) became the present nave (whic function had previously been performed by th north aisle). In the 50 years or so that follow the restoration many donors helped to embelli the church with painted glass and sundry fi tings. The authorities had made use of one the best Victorian architects; one cannot he wishing the congregation had followed the example instead of choosing such second-ra

raftsmen. The west window of the south aisle
(after Holman Hunt) is a special shock.

4

ARISH CHURCH OF ST PETER

t Peter's Street   13th Century

iewed from across the road, this church and its
urrounding buildings might be the kernel of any
nglish village. The church, with its well-kept
ard, is adjoined by a half-timbered house [cf.

John Boys' House (37)] with a blocked Tudor
door frame. Across the lane is a pub with a name
one might expect to find beside a village green,
and in the near distance the Georgian manor
[St Peter's House (56)]. St Peter's is another
3-aisled hall church, built of flint, stone and the
inevitable Roman bricks. The lower part of the
tower, though obviously extremely ancient,
hardly qualifies as Anglo-Saxon. Within, the
round arch at the west end of the north arcade

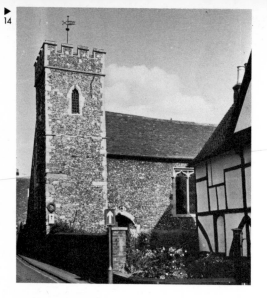

bears witness of a Norman church. The arch into the tower (just inside the door) is Early English as are the arcades, which repeat the rural quality of the exterior to give the impression of a remote, unmolested country church. A decorated Easter sepulchre pierces the north wall of the sanctuary; in both Decorated and Perpendicular periods the windows were remodelled, but neither programme affected the main fabric. Two lancets enigmatically pierce the south arcade wall; was this once an exterior wall? If so, the appearance of the tower arch suggests the south aisle was added very soon afterwards. There are ceiled crown post roofs throughout.

15

PARISH CHURCH OF ST STEPHEN
Hackington   13th Century

Although a church has stood here since the early Saxon period, the earliest work remaining dates from *c.* 1100, when St Anselm rebuilt it and appears in the lower parts of the west tower (see Norman windows on each side). After that additions and changes were made continually throughout the Middle Ages. The tower now has a slightly pointed transitional west door richly adorned with chevron moulding, and in the later Middle Ages had small Perpendicular belfry openings and sturdy angle buttresses added. On top is a curiously designed, but attractive, spire. Within the Perpendicular south porch is a Norman doorway surmounted by a diapered tympanum. The arch is turned with a roll moulding supported by engaged shafts and cushion capitals. The aisle-less nave has one Norman window and two lancets in the north wall and three lancets in the south wall (*c.* 1225). All are deeply splayed inside, indicating a thick Norman wall. The roof is ceiled. At the crossing are Norman semi-circular transept arches of unusual width. They must belong to the transitional period and may be constructed of re-used Norman stones. The transepts themselves were Early English (see blocked lancet in west wall of south transept).

The chancel interior is typically Early English with wide lancet windows and engaged shafts stained black to resemble Purbeck marble. Externally the chancel shows a major remodelling of the late 14th century, which filled the lancets with Perpendicular tracery, added the neat lines of buttresses, and culminated in the noble east window in which formal trefoiled panels contrive to produce intersecting ogee arches. A later restoration was made *c.* 1563 by Sir Roger Manwood, founder of the nearby hospital (33). He rebuilt the south transept in brick and had placed there his fine tomb, by Maximilian Colt (*c.* 1592). Sir Roger's skeleton lies on a pallet

16

BLACKFRIARS   13th and 14th Centuries
Blackfriars Street

Two buildings on opposite banks of the Stour remain of this friary, begun in 1237. To the east is the Frater (now the Christian Science

Church) built of flint and stone; Early English doorways remain, while most of the windows are Decorated. It is well worth going inside to see the upper storey under its timber roof and the vault of the undercroft, the ribs of which were rebuilt with brick in the later Middle Ages. The building across the river is known as the Dominican Guest House (at present the College of Art refectory), though it is not certain what function it actually served. Though now completely restored, evidence remains of Decorated features including a large east window.

17
CHURCH OF ST MARGARET
St Margaret's Street   **14th Century**
A 3-aisled hall church of flint and stone. The exterior was completely restored by Sir Gilbert Scott c. 1850, when the chancel was reduced to its polygonal apse form to leave room for widening the road. The Norman church that stood here is commemorated by a door at the west end in the style of the mid-12th century, and the rest of the church and tower follows the Perpendicular rebuilding of c. 1380. The apse forms a charming composition with its delicate decorated tracery and crockets, more usually found on a sculptural rather than architectural scale in England.

18
PARISH CHURCH OF ST DUNSTAN
                        14th and 15th Centuries
St Dunstan's Street
This 2-aisled church was founded late in the 11th century, but the only part of the flint masonry which could be Norman is the north

wall. The chapel by the north porch dates from c. 1330, and the rest is Perpendicular (though much restored), the tower and single 4-bay arcade within being fine examples of this style. The south Chapel of St. Nicholas (1402) is built of brick laid in English bond. Within it are the tombs of the Roper family [Roper's Gate (32) nearby] and beneath a slab, inscribed recently by the Anglican authorities *Ecclesia Anglicana libera sit*, lies the head of St Thomas More (Sir Thomas to Anglicans) retrieved from London Bridge by his daughter, Margaret Roper, in 1535.

19
CHURCH OF THE HOLY CROSS   **1380**
Westgate
The original church of this dedication was over the earlier Westgate. The present flint church was begun in 1380 by Archbishop Simon of

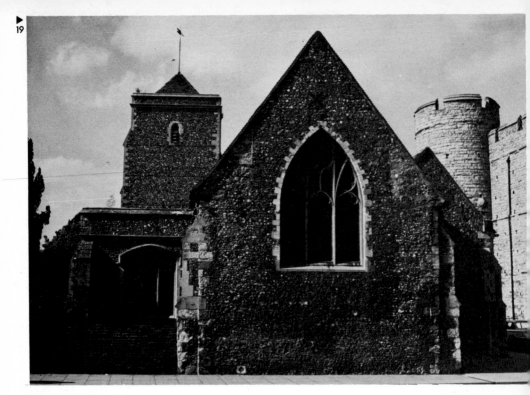

Sudbury (1375–81) – ill-fated victim of Wat Tyler – when the old Westgate was demolished. Little remains of great interest owing to heavy restoration. The east window of the nave is still narrow and sharply pointed, but the delicate Decorated tracery is treated with Perpendicular logic [see St Alphege (12), north aisle]. A more complex example of this can be seen in the east window of St Stephen's, Hackington (15). A tall north aisle extends alongside the nave as far as the chancel. The tower rises from the north-west corner. The walled graveyard, reached through the church, provides a surprisingly rural retreat. The church is presently the Ecumenical Chaplaincy of the University of Kent.

20
HOSPITAL FOR POOR PRIESTS c. 1370
Stour Street

Founded early in the 12th century as a hospital for aged and unbeneficed priests. The present building of flint and stone was erected under the mastership of Thomas Wyke. Since the dissolution of the monasteries the hospital has served a number of useful functions including those of workhouse, Bluecoat school; police station, and is now a welfare clinic.

21
WESTGATE c. 1380
The Westgate probably stands on the site of a Roman defensive gate. It was almost certainly designed by Henry Yevele [see also Castle (4) and Cathedral (5)] in about 1380, a writ of aid for re-walling the city having been granted by the Crown in 1378. Two 60-ft drum towers flank a square-framed arch. The height of the towers between plinth and parapet is bisected by a string course, but this line is not continued across the middle section either by the top of the gateway or the machicolation above it. Nor is the crenellation continuous across the whole. Thus a syncopation is produced that relieves what Christopher Hohler has aptly called the 'fearful symmetry of military architecture' of this date. By about 1430 threats to the city's defences had grown considerably less, and the towers being as difficult to escape from as to enter, they became a city gaol for the next 400 years.

CITY WALL
Restored 14th Century and later

Based on Roman foundations, the city wall was completed by the reign of Richard I. Considerable renovations were carried out in the 1380s under Richard II, with Henry Yevele, architect of the Cathedral nave, keeping a watchful eye on the masonry. The material is rubble faced with flint and strengthened with stone. The wall is 1½ miles long and originally had six main entrances: Northgate, Burgate, Newingate, Ridingate, Worthgate and Westgate. Only the Westgate remains (21), but most of the 21 bastions are still intact, though some of them are embedded in later buildings. Amongst them are the Bastion Chapel (Broad Street, entered from the Kent War Memorial), the Sudbury Tower and no. 16 (both in Pound Lane). Half the wall stands today; stretches run parallel with Broad Street and with the ring road

from Pin Hill to Upper and Lower Bridge Street.

23
HOUSE IN CHURCH LANE
Off St Radigund's Street   **14th Century**
A half-timbered house with brick nogging, some of it plastered. Originally a Wealden house it has been much modified, being at one time a hostelry and at present the Department of Dress and Textiles of the College of Art.

24
THE CHEQUER OF THE HOPE
            14th Century
Corner of High Street and Mercery Lane
The stone-built arcaded ground floor is all that remains of the once much larger Chequer of the Hope (its name deriving from the 'chequer' of land on which it stands). It is now used as a tobacconist's shop. Like Messrs Hepworth's diagonally opposite, it was an inn for pilgrims and is, of course, said to have entertained Chaucer (who often visited Canterbury in his capacity as a Clerk of Works responsible for supervising the renovation of the defences). Across Mercery Lane, Boots the Chemists have an interesting mediæval cellar (as do other premises in the area); it is on two levels, one above the other, the lower one being a rib-vaulted chamber two bays square with a well in one corner.

25
44 IVY LANE   **14th Century**
A perfect example of a Wealden house, with characteristic jettied upper floors flanking the central hall. The house runs parallel to the street and has recently been restored by Anthony Swaine.

26
THE MASTER'S LODGE   **14th Century**
EASTBRIDGE HOSPITAL
St Peter's Street
This house was much remodelled in the 16th,

17th and 18th centuries, and was restored recently by Anthony Swaine to reveal its 14th-century timber construction and Tudor and 18th-century brickwork, the Victorian wing being totally removed and a mediæval double timber window (from a demolished building) being added. It is the private residence of the Master of the Eastbridge Hospital [or St Thomas Hospital (3)]. Its gateway affords a glimpse of a little-known corner of Canterbury, hidden by high walls and street fronts, through which the Stour gently flows, and where quite an astonishing picture of past centuries is evoked. The area is best seen from a small boat on the river.

FALSTAFF INN 15th Century

St Dunstan's Street

This inn was originally built, like many others, to house pilgrims and still performs more or less the same task (even if the pilgrimage is now a photographic one for many visitors). Standing just without the walls it was useful to those who arrived after the curfew. The building is now 17th century in character, having those pleasant windows with arched transoms that are most notably seen in Sparrow's House in Ipswich.

ALL SAINTS' COURT Late 15th Century

All Saints' Lane, off St Peter's Street

Built over the flagstones of an 11th-century governor's residence, the present building is typical of a late 15th-century Kentish merchant's house. The frontage, revealed in 1931, has a fine collection of carved brackets, originally from Lady Wootton's Priory – supporting the bressumer below the jettied upper storey. This upper storey was constructed as one great chamber, 77 × 18 ft. Of special interest: a parchment-weave window of *c.* 1450; a fine staircase of 1510; a collection of large Sussex fireplaces dating from 1567. The house is now a private residence.

PARISH CHURCH OF ST MILDRED
16th Century and earlier

Church Lane (extension of Stour Street)

The oldest foundation within the city walls and one of Canterbury's 2-aisled hall churches [cf. St Alphege (12)]. The tower was demolished in 1832, and the nave and chancel are of equal height, presenting a long, low composition when viewed from the south. The west and

▶
27

south walls of the nave are largely Anglo-Saxon work of rubble, flint and a few Roman bricks. The south-west and south-east corners of the nave have megalithic Saxon quoins; they are over 60 feet apart and suggest the existence of a large and important pre-Conquest church. The rest of the building is rather uninteresting Perpendicular, though the south Chapel of Our Lady of 1512 is a good example of flint and stone chequer work. Inside, the nave and north aisle are not divided by a proper arcade, for there is only one actual column (Perpendicular, octagonal section with hollowed sides), the other arches merely piercing the wall. In the chancel the arches have double flat chamfers, but in the nave they are hollow and probably later [cf. St Alphege (12) for a complete version of this type of arcade]. The roofs are of crown post construction, which is typical of Canterbury.

TOWER OF THE CHURCH OF ST MARY MAGDALENE   *c.* 1502
Burgate

Only the tower remains of the church, which was demolished in 1871. Built of stone repaired with flint, it is divided into three storeys by two string courses and capped with a squat pyramid-shaped roof. The arches that led into nave and aisle remain open to reveal memorials

preserved from the church, including a fine monument to John Whitfield (died 1691).

31
CHRISTCHURCH GATE   1517
Buttermarket

A splendid point of inflection between the snugness of Mercery Lane and the grandeur of the Cathedral Precincts. A 4-centred main arch, with smaller gateway for pedestrians alongside, is surmounted by the inscription: *Hoc opus constructum est Anno Domini millesimo quingentesimo septimo* (*decimo*). Above this rise two enclosed storeys below which runs a band of heraldic blazons, and between which is a frieze of angels holding shields painted with a variety of Christian symbols. Over the main gateway is a Tudor rose between the arms of Henry VIII and Katherine of Aragon. Atop all this are battlements and pinnacles restored to their original appearance. The whole façade is covered with blind Perpendicular tracery. The fine niche once held a statue of Christ. The entrance passage has a star vault with heraldic bosses and a great Tudor rose in the midst. The oak doors of 1660 bear the arms of their donor, Archbishop Juxon (1660–3).

32
ROPER'S GATE   16th Century
St Dunstan's Street

All that remains of Place House, home of Margaret Roper (daughter of Sir Thomas More), and an interesting example of Tudor brickwork. The courses are laid in English bond and much use is made of moulded brick. A 4-centred brick arch is surmounted by a square surround, and above this is a 3-light rectangular window set in a stepped gable. Further embellishment is provided by two raised lozenges and an oculus in the apex of the gable.

SIR ROGER MANWOOD'S HOSPITAL
c. 1570

St Stephen's Green, Hackington

This pleasant line of almshouses, facing the village green, was founded and endowed for the aged poor *c.* 1573 by Sir Roger Manwood, Justice of the Queen's Bench and later to become Chief Baron of the Exchequer. The hospital consists of six houses of standard collegiate type built of brick laid in English bond and decorated with a large chequer pattern across the front in dark brick. The ends of the row are embellished with stepped gables. At the south-west end is Ye Olde Beverlie, originally the larger house of the Clerk of the Parish who was also warden of the hospital. After lengthy sermons ale was served in the Warden's Lodging, and in the process of time it became a pleasant village inn, which character it still possesses. The hospital was handsomely restored in the 1930s.

34

PARKER'S GATE   16th Century
Palace Street

Built of flint with brick window dressings, this was the gatehouse to the Palace rebuilt by Archbishop Matthew Parker, first archbishop of Queen Elizabeth I's reign, in the third quarter of the 16th century. It has since been completely restored and enlarged.

35

WESTGATE GROVE   Late 16th Century

A good chance is here provided to see from a distance a late mediæval street front at its best. Well looked after, these houses are a charming example of the sort of building that still gives Canterbury its essential character. Sir John

▶
32

Falstaff would have felt nearly as much at home here as in his eponymous inn across the road [Falstaff Inn (27)].

36
THE WEAVERS 16th Century
St Peter's Street
These mid-16th-century half-timbered houses have been completely restored, but give a good impression of what much of Canterbury must have looked like. Originally they were occupied by Huguenots and Walloons, many of whom fled here from persecution and set up a major weaving industry in the city.

37
SIR JOHN BOYS' HOUSE c. 1600
Palace Street
Now the King's School Shop, this Tudor house of c. 1600 was the property of the Canterbury

lawyer and philanthropist, Sir John Boys (1535–1612), who founded the Jesus Hospital for the aged poor in the Northgate. It is timber framed but with no visible diagonal or curved bracing. Much of the parged nogging takes the form of rustication. Only the fanciful corner brackets below the first two jettied floors break away from the severe geometrical form of the building. The north elevation presents an intricate rectilinear composition in black and white which would probably have delighted the modern artist, Mondrian; the front door would probably have not.

38
QUEEN ELIZABETH'S GUEST CHAMBER 16th and 17th Century
High Street
The florid pargetting on the upper floor, with cartouches at each end and putti seated on barrels among swirling vines – referring to the

37

fact that this is an inn – dates from the 17th century. The overhanging bays, in 17th-century manner, are early 20th-century restorations, and with the clumsy plaster rustication give the façade a rather phoney appearance. Besides the pargetting, the best feature of the building is the robust 16th-century plaster ceiling in the solar on the first floor. It com-prises an ingenious pattern of interlocking circles, linked by heavy bosses, some of which include the Tudor rose and the royal initials E.R., lending some colour to the tradition that Queen Elizabeth I entertained the Duke of Alençon here in 1573. The butcher's shop on the ground floor preserves a whole wall of Victorian murals in sepia-toned tiles.

39
HOUSE OF AGNES   Mid-17th Century
St Dunstan's Street

Described by Dickens as 'bulging out over the road, . . . beams with carved ends and heads bulging out too, so that I fancied the whole house was hanging forward, trying to see who was passing on the narrow pavement below', though the tradition that this is the building which Dickens had in mind in describing Agnes Wickfield's house in *David Copperfield* is not wholly unimpeachable. Thirteen successive gables recall the appearance of the street in the 17th century, in spite of later alterations. This is the best survivor of that date with hanging pendants, arched transoms to the bay windows and a naive segmental pediment interrupting the fascia board over the entrance.

40
16 WATLING STREET   1625

Described by E. Hasted in 1799 as a 'large venerable mansion . . . built in the first year of the reign of Charles I'. Its neighbours to the left, until the 1942 bombings, were two Dutch gabled houses which bore the same date, 1625. English bond brickwork, stone quoins and vertical lacings, the shallow arched form of the ground floor windows, and Doric entablature all conform with an early 17th-century date. The house stands on splendid vaulted cellars. The coroneted chimney pot may record the Prince and Princess of Orange's visit to this house in

1677. The building was greatly altered, first in 1725 with the introduction of sash windows, the addition of a parapet, and stable wing at the rear. Further modifications seem to have been carried out on a change of ownership in 1803 when the large Regency-type windows were installed at the back, arrd what was probably a fine pedimented portico was replaced by the present inadequate porch. This is one of the best old houses in Canterbury and would much benefit from restoration.

41
CAROLEAN COTTAGE   1627
7 Ivy Lane

A delightful little cottage distinguished by a steep 'cat-slide' roof with a picturesque ripple. There is some fine timbering inside. The date inscribed at the side, with initials and a heart, may refer to a change of ownership rather than to the building of the cottage, and perhaps to a reconstruction at that time.

42
JOHN SMITH'S HOSPITAL   1656-7
Longport

Endowed by John and Ann Smith in gratitude for the birth of a son in 1644, after 20 years of childless marriage, the hospital provided dwellings for four poor men and four poor women. The iron figures '1657' under the shaped gables provide a distinctive decorative feature. Unlike some other almshouses, there are no communal buildings or chapel provided, merely

tiny front gardens and some land at the rear. The buildings are of great charm, with their wooden shutters, brick modillion cornice and tall chimneys. They are at present undergoing modernisation, to provide less cramped quarters for four people, and it is to be hoped that the chimneys will be preserved.

43
6–8 BEST LANE   17th Century
The pair, nos. 6 and 7, are distinguished by a pleasant use of black brick with red brick quoining. The projecting string course and modillion frieze lend them a dignified appearance, and indicate their late 17th-century origin. No. 8 needs some attention and it is to be hoped that any restoration will preserve the original window mullion divisions, now lost by its twin. Despite the sash windows of a later period, no. 6 is earlier than its neighbours as is suggested by the overhang and high-pitched gable. The façade, hung with alternate scallop and chevron tiles, would be much improved by the removal of its present coat of paint.

44
THE MANOR HOUSE Late 17th Century
101 St Stephen's Road
Next door to Glebe House (48), and contrasting strongly with the obsessive symmetry and orderliness of that building. The setting is informal, with a rambling 17th-century mews to the right, now converted into cottages, and the house equally so with irregularly spaced windows, the upper ones crammed up under the eaves, and an off-centre porch added at a later date in a fortunately vain attempt to make the structure more sophisticated.

45
70–4 BROAD STREET 13th–18th Century
A group of domestic buildings with the juxtaposition of varied colour, texture and style so characteristic of Canterbury. The roof of no. 7

is as early as the 13th century; its interior dates from the 15th century. The squatness and irregularity contrast dramatically with the 18th-century proportion of no. 71, which sports a handsome pedimented doorway with panelled reveals, and must date from the 1780s. New brickwork over the adjacent window, and that window's proportion suggest that a shop was intended here. To the left, nos. 72–4, high and narrow with steep gables, provide a further contrast. The deep-set doors are original and the ground and first floors have good brickwork in Flemish bond, dated 1693, though no. 73's pebble-dashed gable is regrettable.

20 KING STREET

Late 17th–early 18th Century

Not rectangular in plan as the façade suggests, but L-shaped to accommodate the boundary of St Alphege's graveyard. The foundations seem to be mediæval. It was used as a public house around 1800, when the windows were reduced in number and altered to Regency proportions, but Anthony Swaine has recently sensitively restored the original appearance. The unsatisfactory scale of the round-headed window and the break in the string course imply that a more flamboyant portal probably succumbed to the 1787 Lighting and Paving Act. The interior is partially timbered.

47

62 BURGATE   **1725**

A fine house illustrating the crisp virtues of good red brick and tall sash windows. The profiled string courses and drip moulds are characteristic of the finesse of the earlier 18th century, and contrast with the more robust quality of mid-Georgian work [cf. Westgate House (55)]. The rear of the house has been

46

much altered. The staircase is wood panelled. The rain heads bear the date 1725.

48
GLEBE HOUSE Early–Mid 18th Century
St Stephen's Green
Previously the rectory of St Stephen's church, the house is distinguished by an unusually elaborate carved wood portal. Fluted Doric pilasters are surmounted by capitals with the canonical rosettes decorating the neck, egg and dart borrowed from the Ionic on the echinus, Ionic again for the architrave with overlapping fasciæ, and back to Doric for the triglyph frieze. A nice spray is carved in the pediment. The interior is spacious, with a particularly large hall, the pattern of which is repeated at first-floor level, where a concealed 'hole' big enough for a fugitive still exists.

49
59–63 CASTLE STREET
Mediæval and 18th Century
A well kept row of mediæval cottages given a new front probably early in the 18th century and fortunately virtually untouched since

then. Utterly simple but attractive to look at.

50
BARTON COURT now TECHNICAL HIGH SCHOOL FOR GIRLS   1740–50
Longport

The Manor of Barton, which belonged to St Augustine's at the time of the Domesday Book, dates from a Saxon charter of 833. The present building, described in 1774 by W. Gostling as a 'handsome mansion house', is the standard Flemish bond, five bays and two storeys, with hipped roof and dormers. The bays at each end make the two front ground floor rooms very

light and spacious. The doorway has banded rustication on the pilasters echoed in the rusticated Palladian window above, which is cramped and lacks Burlingtonian solidarity. [See also (109).]

51
THE BUTTERMARKET
Mediæval and 18th Century

By the 12th century it was laid out more or less in its present form; the site has served as Bullstake, Buttermarket and theatre, but has been dominated by Christchurch Gate since 1517. It provides an intimate point of contact between the sacred and the secular, an intimacy enhanced by the random juxtaposition of styles in its buildings. The Olive Branch public house has a pleasant Georgian shop-front, but the Regency frontage of the Cathedral Gate Hotel, adjoining Christchurch Gate, which still expresses the mediæval overhang, is better still, and has excellent neo-classical detail.

52
THE PRESBYTERY

59 Burgate   **Mediæval and 18th Century**

A mediæval house, refurbished in the 18th century with new windows, the addition of

a sturdy doorway with Doric columns and entablature, and by a fluted 'frieze' to the edge of the overhang. The upper floors are faced with mathematical tiles imitating the brickwork on street level. The hall and staircase, sacrificing living space to 'spaciousness', also reflect the ideals of the 18th century.

53
11 THE PRECINCTS Mid-18th Century
The interior is now spoiled by division into flats, but there are interesting ceilings on the ground floor, diamond patterned with slim carved wood strips. There is no reason to

suppose the octagonal projection over the porch, supported on wooden Tuscan columns, a later addition.

54
ST DUNSTAN'S HOUSE
Mediæval and 1750
Varied window proportions make a pleasing and unusual feature for a house whose front was remodelled in the mid-18th century. The house dates at least from the 16th century, as is more evident from the back, though it has been suggested that it may be as early as the 12th century. Tantalising fragments of 15th-century wall painting survive in several rooms.

55
WESTGATE HOUSE   1760
87 St Dunstan's Street
An imposing four-square mid-Georgian house, dated on the rainheads. The garden front is enlivened by a central Venetian window and there is another at the end of the projecting stable block. The interior is spacious and largely original, but of no special merit, apart from a rococo overmantel in one of the ground-floor rooms. It has the simple virtues of good building and good proportions.

56
ST PETER'S HOUSE   Mid-18th Century
St Peter's Lane
A mellow red bricked house, dating from at least 1752, ends the deep vista down narrow St Peter's Lane. Its broad façade belies its shallow depth, in a way more typical of later landscaped architecture, though in this case it

arises from the nature of the site. Otherwise entirely plain, the broken pedimented doorway with simple fanlight provides the only emphasis.

57
BARTON MILL   Late 18th Century
Sturry Road

The Domesday Book records a mill on this site and until the dissolution it belonged to the monks of Christ Church. The present buildings form an attractive group with the 4-storey weather-boarded structure straddling the Stour and the late 18th-century houses enclosing a small yard. It must have been the mill owner at that time, one Allen Grebell, who also built c. 1780 the large and handsome house, midway between the river and the road, as his own residence. Hopefully, the present owners will find means to rescue this fine building from its present dereliction.

▶
56

▶
57

1–5 LONDON ROAD
Late 18th–early 19th Century

An exemplary group showing the development of domestic building from late Georgian to Regency: plain brick articulated only by string courses and pedimented doorways (no. 1); painted keying courses over the windows (no. 2); a touch of individualism in the recessed arcade (no. 3); and then a pair with rendered façades whose 'thermal' windows and redundant mock-keystones are the solecisms of a builder with pretentions, but a mockery of the classical vocabulary.

59
36 ST MARGARET'S STREET — 1770

A handsome little building whose modest cornice is just right for a house of this size. The elegant shallow bows, divided by mullions into three lights, look like a Regency modification.

60
THE HOYSTINGS — 18th–19th Century
Old Dover Road

The name remains enigmatic, but dates at least from the 16th century and refers to the place rather than the house, which is mid-18th-century red-brick, Gothicised half-way through the following century, judging from the style of the additions at the rear. The tracery lights are graceful enough, but the doorway is insensitive stock builders' stuff. The stepped gables of the dormers are contemporary with the alterations, and are still more quaintly eclectic. Inside, the stairwell is lit by a tall Gothic window, over-hung by a heavy ceiling with Gothic mouldings, furnished with cast iron bannisters with pointed arches. All this is in conflict with the classical columns supporting the upper landing, and the whole staircase is on a scale quite disproportionate with the size of the house.

61
DON JON TERRACE — 1800–5

At the east end of Dane John Gardens, where

59

58

tevenson's 'Invicta' steam-engine now stands, this is an attractive terrace with slated mansard roofs, an unusual feature in Canterbury at this period. At the right are two 3-bay houses whose façades are modulated by a sophisticated use of pilasters and a shallow break-forward of the central feature into which the doors are deeply recessed. Modest use of an abbreviated key-pattern below the ground-floor windows dignifies their narrower, but deeper neighbours. Built during the first years of the century, if Gostling's 1805 map is to be trusted.

62
6–19 KING STREET
Early 19th Century
King Street, Blackfriars Street and Mill Lane form a compact little group of artisan cottages dating from the years around the turn of the century. Their charm lies in their intimacy, the scale of the buildings matching the width of these narrow streets, whose atmosphere remains countrified rather than metropolitan. This little group is distinguished by the clever way each pair of doors, with their tiny lunettes, is embraced within a single elliptical arch.

63
CANTERBURY PRISON   **1808**
Longport
Architect: George Byfield
Completed in 1808 as the 'County Gaol and House of Correction' in the grounds of St Augustine's. In 1813, *The Gentleman's Magazine* described George Byfield, a pupil of Robert Taylor, as 'an eminent architect who has built

several gaols and for many years has made this branch of his profession his particular study.' Its immediate predecessor was Bury St Edmunds Gaol, built in 1803, with which Byfield was connected. Both structures are very early examples of the radiating plan which derives from Jeremy Bentham's 'Panopticon' or radiating plan published in 1791 and developed in his proposals for a National Penitentiary. The forceful stone façade is expressive of its function with heavy rock-faced rustication round the massive entrance topped by a grilled lunette. The two bastions – that on the right incised with Byfield's name – add to the fortress-like effect.

64
SESSIONS HOUSE   **1808**
Longport
Architect: George Byfield

Designed immediately after the Prison (63) on an adjoining site; prisoners were conveyed between the two buildings by a subterranean passage. It has several Greek revival features, being uncompromisingly planned as a cubic mass, with giant Doric columns *in antis* surmounted by oversize mutules like those of the Prison. It is handsomely faced in Portland stone ashlar, and the symbols of justice and authority are echoed in the original iron railings which embrace the two buildings. It was said that two figures of 'Justice' and 'Mercy' occupied a position in the 19th century above the doorway. The central window contributes a touch of domesticity to an otherwise suitably chilling façade. If the figures stood there, rather than above the entablature, they would have partially concealed this feature. Hasted found the Sessions House 'equal if not superior to any other in the kingdom'. [See also (115).]

ST PETER'S METHODIST CHAPEL 1811
Off St Peter's Street
Architect: William Jenkins of Lambeth
Two architects of the name Jenkins, father and
son, are recorded. The father, who died in 1844,
was a Methodist itinerant preacher as well as an
architect. Whether he or his son designed this
building is unclear, but one or other was responsible for many Methodist chapels including
those at nearby Rochester (1810) and at Bath
(Walcot Chapel, 1815). The latter, though more
elaborate, has a number of features specifically
in common with the Canterbury building including the small forecourt, the pedimented
3-bay projection and flanking recessed bays,
and the central windows in recessed margins.
All these structures are of a generic type going
back to Wesley's City Road Chapel of 1778.
The yellow London stocks of the façade (the
sides are in cheaper, red brick) have kept a warm
appearance too often obliterated in the grime of
the metropolis. The design is simple, in accord-
ance with Methodist principles, but elegant,
with tactful use of stone in the string courses,
and of tall round-headed windows with, apart
from two exceptions, their original slim glazing

bars. The portico is unobtrusive because it is
perfectly in scale. The interior originally had an
oval gallery supported on slim iron columns, but
during recent modernisation this was cut back
to form a hemicycle, creating a somewhat
theatrical effect. The builder, William Moss,
may also be the local architect of the same name,
which could account for the sympathy with
which Jenkins' design has been handled. The
brickwork is exemplary and in excellent repair.

66
THEATRE now REDIFFUSION
OFFICES 1789–90 and 1815
Orange Street
Originally Canterbury's first theatre: built by
Mrs Sarah Baker, the most successful circuit
proprietor of the day, when the building over
the Buttermarket, used as a theatre, was demolished. It was erected on the site of an older
concert room and was on the same economical
rectangular plan, and quite plain, as were her
nine other theatres in Kent. In 1815 when a
certain Mr Dowton took over, large sums were
spent on embellishments, such as an elaborately
painted ceiling, now gone, with the rest of the
original interior, and the present façade was

constructed. The ground floor with its engaged Greek Doric columns and chamfering is undistinguished, but above, the tall tapering windows and their surrounds reflect the currently fashionable style of the Greek revival, and may have influenced the similar feature used a few years later on the now mutilated Museum and Philosophical Institution in Guildhall Street. Nineteenth-century guides consistently refer to this feature of both buildings as 'Egyptian', but whereas its origins are to be found in Vitruvius' description of Greek building practice, its use here is characteristic merely of provincial eclecticism. Nevertheless, taken together with the moulded aprons, the shallow recessed margin of the central window and the lunette above it makes an attractive composition.

67

THE ELMS   1820
17 Old Dover Road
Architect: G. Moss

Though there seems to have been a building here from 1750, the present handsome house, from the evidence of a signed drawing, probably dates from 1820. The chamfered rustication of the ground floor and the very broad and splendid fanlight, which stretches almost the whole width of the hall inside, lend distinction to an otherwise plain façade. There are some good mouldings and fireplaces, using Adam motifs, on the first floor. For the work of an obscure local architect the design is a sophisticated one,

▶
66

▶▶
67

with services housed in the projection at the rear. The house, which now presents a bleak appearance, could be much improved if the rendering was painted as intended, and if the shutters to the upper floor windows, visible in old photographs, were replaced.

68

ZOAR CHAPEL   *c.* 182?
Burgate Lane

When St George's Gate with its water tower was demolished in 1801, the round bastion which now forms the chancel of this little chapel was transformed into a storage cistern. A square block attached to the bastion existed at least as early as 1800, and the present building certainly pre-dates the arrival of the Zoar Baptists in 1845. The miniature scale (the brickwork appropriately Flemish bond) is in keeping with the scale of the lane, yet the architectural features are few and bold – three semi-circular openings with fanlights, linked and emphasised by broad bands of painted cement.

69

15–23 DON JON GROVE   182?
Dane John Gardens

The Gardens were laid out in 1790, their focal point being the curious conical mound, of contested purpose and antiquity, standing near the city wall. In 1834 the Gardens were the subject of a charming, if lengthy poem, 'moral, sentimental and complimentary' by the local writer G. F. Bennett, who characterised them as the site where 'our stripling peasantry convene For hale gymnastics on the Sylvan scene.' The builder of this terrace has clearly taken his site into account – like Nash's Regent's Park terraces, these are buildings to be seen, and sit in a similar landscaped setting. A vein of eclectic fantasy characteristic of the period is apparent in the Gothicised façade of the central house. This stands at the right hand of a group of three, and it would be interesting to know whether it is a later alteration or an original

eature in response to a patron's request. The easy transition from giant pilaster order to octagonal turrets, the structural consistency of the crenellated parapet with the shallow segmental arch motif carried along from the left, the whole concept of building as surface treatment, of the façade as a theatrical backdrop, argues at least for its original status.

70
4–18 MONASTERY STREET
Between 1825 and 1843
A simple terrace of cottages, restored by L. R. Barlow so that the pretty fluted door jambs and the delicate brackets supporting the rain shelters are seen to best advantage.

71
26 CASTLE STREET *c.* **1825–35**
An elegant Regency façade concealing a modest mediæval dwelling, whose dormers just show over the parapet. Shallow bays conform with Canterbury's 1787 Lighting and Paving Act, which permitted ground-floor projections of no more than 12 inches. Illusions of grandeur are created by the extension of the façade over

service entrance and carriage way. Inside, the house is only one room deep. There is a chaste use of classicising decorative motifs: the apron over the service entrance [see Theatre (66)], and the key-pattern incised in the stucco over the central bay on the first floor [see the smaller houses in Don Jon Terrace (61)].

72
THANINGTON HOUSE   *c.* 183
140 Wincheap

Originally a modest 2-storey house, its second floor and extensions at the rear were added in about 1830. The rather clumsy hoods over the first-floor windows may be later still, but they give piquancy to an otherwise undistinguished façade. The back of the house is clad in mathematical tiles in imitation of the brickwork at the sides. There are three mid-18th-century tomb stones let into the floor of the cellar.

73
2–20 ST DUNSTAN'S TERRACE
1832 and later

Canterbury's 'suburbs' – those parts of the town outside the walls – expanded considerably during the late 18th and early 19th century, not least due to a large military contingent quartered nearby. This terrace, and 24 and 25 Orchard Street, were put up by a speculative builder after the threat of invasion had passed, but with an eye to the continuing military presence. Another century passed before the terrace became one side of a street, the land opposite having been protected from development at the time of building. The buildings are essentially plain, but enlivened by their trappings of louvered shutters and elegantly designed wrought-iron balconies, some of which have unfortunately been lost. The 3-storey houses at each end have bow windows, and gently pitched roofs with overhanging eaves; the 2-storey cottages have recessed blank panels above the upper floor windows and bays below.

74
WAREHOUSES
Pound Lane   **2nd quarter of 19th Century**
On the site of the old city wall near Westgate,

this section of which was demolished *c.* 1825. The structure on the right, taken together with Greenfield Cottages (91) represents a 19th-century local vernacular with its half-hearted chequer in flint and ragstone – perhaps in both cases stemming from the availability of old building materials.

75
WEST STATION   1845–6
Station Road

This is not the station built to serve Stevenson's first steam passenger line, Canterbury to Whitstable, in 1830, whose terminus was in North Lane, but a building put up when the London and Dover Railway reached Canterbury on its way to Ramsgate. One of the more modest among early neo-classical stations, this is a 1-storey stucco building with fluted baseless Greek Doric columns *in antis*. The *Illustrated London News* reported 'the roof of the station is of Iron, it is a peculiarly light and graceful construction.' Sadly the platform is now covered by a modern roof more utilitarian than elegant, and the portico has been defaced by black paint.

favourite architect, Butterfield rejected the 'late' Gothic of the Commissioners' Churches and returned to the earlier and more robust 'middle-pointed' style. The buildings, occupying three sides of the outer court of the ruined Abbey, stand mainly over mediæval foundations. (The remains of the 11th-century Abbey church lie uncovered just beyond.) They include the restored early 14th-century Fyndon's Gate with its fine, lofty upper chamber; a vaulted cloister (north range) now unfortunately subdivided and its reticulated tracery filled with glass; the magnificent Library, a detached building raised over a vaulted undercroft, with an interior still of impressive proportions despite the loss of the original bookcases and the blocking-in of the stilted tie-beam roof; and the Dining Hall and Chapel (west range), both raised and with fine interiors, the former retaining its original crown post roof and stone chimneypiece. Largely a reconstruction in the original materials of knapped flint and stone dressings, it remains Butterfield's most likeable work, lacking the harshness of his later buildings in banded brick. Hitchcock, with a flash of insight, calls it 'a sort of primitive of the High Victorian'.

77
68 CASTLE STREET   1847
Architect: Hezekiah Marshall
The façade, with its masonry details re-interpreted in brickwork, is still Georgian in character, but the central glazing bars are typically Victorian. The main interest, however, is in the way the building turns the corner with shaped gable after shaped gable (derived from the 17th-century hospital nearby), building up to the climax of the chimney. Marshall refaced and added to an existing house, and the staircase is clearly of an earlier date. The unexpectedly elaborate plaster cornices in the main rooms of the ground floor belong to the new work.

76
ST AUGUSTINE'S COLLEGE   1845-8
Monastery Street
Architect: William Butterfield
The Tractarian Missionary College (since 1969 the 4th Year Ordination Course for King's College, London) was Butterfield's second recorded work, and was followed by his masterpiece, All Saints, Margaret Street, in London. Both works executed under the patronage of that leading high churchman and Member of Parliament, Beresford-Hope. Under the influence of Pugin and as the *Ecclesiologist*'s

78
SYNAGOGUE now ST ALPHEGE
CHURCH HALL   1847–8
King Street
Architect: Hezekiah Marshall

A contemporary made much of the Synagogue being built on land on which had once stood the Hospital of the Knights Templar, but objected to criticism that the style should have been Gothic on the grounds that Jewish religious practices have little in common with Christian. Whether they have any more in common with ancient Egyptian is equally doubtful, but tapering and battered forms had certainly had some currency in Canterbury since the early part of the century [see the Theatre (66), and the traces of the Museum's façade on the east side of Guildhall Street]. The front, in an early example of Portland cement, successfully maintains the scale of a small Egyptian temple (a model of which the architect could have studied in the old Museum) complete with columns and lotus-bud capitals now in need of restoration. Also in need of repair is the charming miniature brick temple in the garden which served as the women's ceremonial baths. The interior, recently restored by Anthony Swaine, must have been impressive before the old furnishings were dispersed.

79
ST STEPHEN'S SCHOOL now PART OF COUNTY PRIMARY SCHOOL 1848
Hackington

The stylistic similarities between the Manwood Almshouse (33) and this little school across the road is appropriate in more ways than one. Its origin was a Dame School which sprung up in one of the almshouses in 1822. Founded and supported for 31 years by the Rev. John White, it remained unaltered until 1908 when the windows were enlarged and extensions built at the west end. Today the quaint flavour of the original can only be appreciated fully in the bell-cote which crowns the school entrance, and in the crow-step gables and diapers of the adjoining house, which provided until recently a home for the headmistress.

80
CHURCH OF   1848–52
ST GREGORY-THE-GREAT
Old Ruttington Lane
Architect: Sir Gilbert Scott

'Carpenter and Butterfield were the apostles of the high-church school – I, of the multitude', said Scott, and certainly this modest flint church with its simple sanctus bell-cote bears out this claim. Almost identical in plan to Pugin's St Mary, Stockton-on-Tees (1842), its different parts – nave, north aisle and chancel – are skilfully brought together in a correct 'middle-pointed' style. The window tracery is particularly convincing, and the church as a whole sits most agreeably in the large and leafy graveyard which served as the burial ground for the whole city. The simplicity is carried into the interior

where the whitewash of the walls and stripped pine of the original pews have replaced the dark Victorian polychromy. A direct hit by a bomb destroyed the stained glass which must have been attractive to judge from the two surviving *grisaille* panels in the chancel.

81
TOWER HOUSE
c. 1380 and Mid-19th Century
Westgate Gardens

A house attached to Archbishop Sudbury's tower [the first city wall bastion south of the

58

Westgate (21[has apparently existed since the 15th century. But the present building with its curious mixture of flint and brick dressings must be early Victorian, and even the tower appears to have been embattled and refaced in flint at that time (a drawing dated 1832 shows a single-storey wing attached to a stone tower with a hipped slate roof). Shaped and crow-step gables were fashionable in Canterbury during the 'forties and 'fifties, and the ruins in the garden were moved probably from St Augustine's c. 1850, all of which suggests that the new house was complete by the early 'fifties. The two additional gabled portions with ornate barge-boards, which were added before 1877, were demolished in 1937 when the house was given by its owner to the city. The building is now the Mayor's parlour, but the beautiful grounds bordering the river Stour are open to everyone, and have so far managed to retain the character of a private garden.

82
MEISTER OMER'S   13th and
The Precincts   mid-19th Century

It is hard to believe that this domestic looking building, now a King's School boarding house, was once a grand mediæval hall in which the Prior entertained his guests. A hint of this remains in the two oriel windows at the east end, part of Prior Chillenden's extensions which broke through the convent wall (1399). The building, named after a monastery official who lived there in the late 13th century, is included here because it looks Victorian rather than mediæval; and there is no doubt, to judge from the roof timbers and from the neat flintwork and stone dressings, that a major reconstruction took place in the 19th century. The repeated use of tall, narrow gables dates from the early 17th century when a second floor was inserted into the upper part of the lofty hall (a first had already encroached on the space in Elizabethan times when the building became a Canon's house). Parts of the old king post roof are still visible on the upper floors, especially where the tie beams rest on carved stone corbels. More impressive survivals, however, are the pointed and richly moulded doorway on the north side (the original entrance), the adjoining polygonal turret with its vice, and the magnificent stone fire-place arch in the kitchen, which spans nearly 22 ft.

83
ORCHARD HOUSE   c. 1852
26 New Street

An uncharacteristic site – shallow and with a long street frontage – has produced an unusual form for a town house. The stable and coach house at one end were put up before 1851 by a previous owner. The house was no doubt designed by its new owner who was a surveyor, and who would have fancied such showmanship as the chamfered rustication of the ground floor and the scrolled pediment over the door. What looks like an urn between the scrolls is in fact the

bust of a girl which was recently re-set back to front.

84
55–69 NEW DOVER ROAD   1853

The exclusive and secretive spaciousness of the Victorian suburb is here seen at its best if the relentless motor traffic can be put out of mind, an act of make-believe which is just possible with the private drive and the magnificent belt of trees. In suburban terms the semi-detached blocks at each end are a portent of things to come, whereas the more impressive central terrace looks back to a Georgian form. But in style it is early 16th century, complicated in silhouette with crow-step gables and chimney clusters; and rich in texture with black diapers set in red brickwork, stone mullioned windows and crocketed hood moulds over the door-ways.

applied to a symmetrical plan with separate sections for boys and girls flanking the headmaster's lodgings in the middle. Whilst economy may have restricted the use of knapped flint and Bath stone dressings to the front and sides (the back is in brick) it did not prevent the architect from indulging in fancy detail like the ornamen-

▶ 85

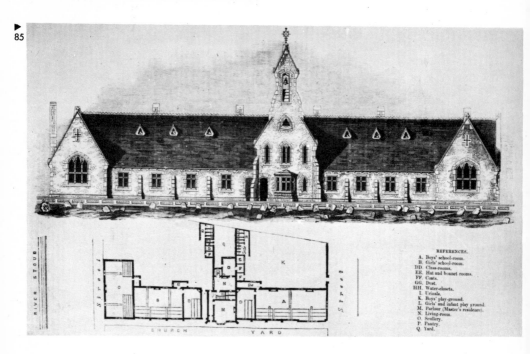

REFERENCES.

A. Boys' school-room.
B. Girls' school-room.
DD. Class-rooms.
EE. Hat and bonnet rooms.
FF. Coats.
GG. Dust.
HH. Water-closets.
I. Urinals.
K. Boys' play-ground.
L. Girls' and infant play ground.
M. Parlour (Master's residence).
N. Living-room.
O. Scullery.
P. Pantry.
Q. Yard.

85
ST MILDRED'S SCHOOL now   **1855**
ORGANBUILDER'S WORKSHOP
Church Lane
Architect: Joseph Messenger
What gives this building its distinctive character is the contrast of tall gables and bell-cote with the low eaves line and steeply pitched roofs. The influences of Butterfield (76) and Scott (80) are obvious, though the picturesque forms are here

tal roof tiling or stone diapers on the chimneys. Though adapted to a new use, the building has been left to deteriorate to a lamentable degree.

86
CLERGY ORPHAN COLLEGE now
ST EDMUND'S SCHOOL   **1854-5**
St Thomas's Hill
Architect: P. C. Hardwick
The first designs (1852) were begun while

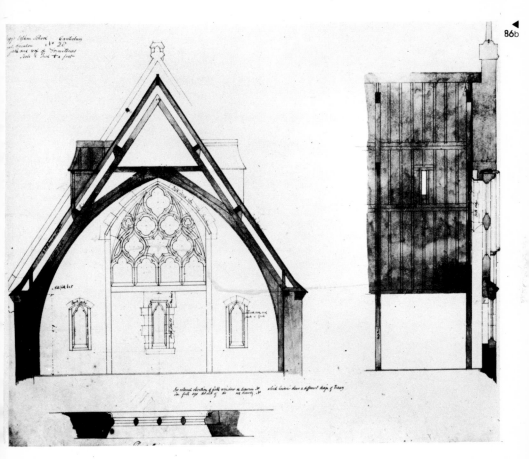

Hardwick was supervising the completion of that strangely prophetic building, the Great Western Hotel. By comparison St Edmund's is eclectic and hardly typical of the time – its lower half English decorated, its upper half French. A wagon roof contains some of the largest dormitories in the world (now sub-divided), effectively lit by a combination of high rose windows and tiny lancets at floor level. The first designs, with the chapel in the middle raised up at first-floor level, explain the prominence of the central block retained by Hardwick even when the dormitories, which had previously flanked the chapel, were carried across. Built of Kentish rag and Bath stone dressings, the building was described by a contemporary writer as plain, due to restrictions of cost. Certainly lack of funds postponed the construction of the chapel (1857), but what strikes one today is the solid pride and all-embracing gesture of the half-H plan astride on the hill. Arthur Blomfield, a former pupil of Hardwick, added the junior house on the north-west side in a plain Tudor style (1897), and his son Charles the French Renaissance building farther to the north (begun 1907). As a partner of Blomfield and Morgan he also carried out a competent enlargement and refurnishing of the chapel (1922–4). More recently a brown brick extension on the north side by Biscoe and Stanton (1967–8) provides a complete contrast while retaining sympathy and respect by its bold forms and articulated junctions.

87
TINTOCH HOUSE now LUXMOORE HOUSE 1860
75 New Dover Road

Now converted into a boarding house for the King's School but originally built by an army general for his own use, this is the typical Victorian villa of the prosperous suburb. The mixture is always the same – an informal grouping of gables and bay windows, an elaborate porch, and the combination of red brick with stone. Some of the details, like the finials over the dormers, or the hopperhead in the shape of a flying dragon, are delightful, and should not be allowed to suffer the same fate as the crudely rebuilt parapets over the bay windows.

88
BAPTIST CHURCH 1863–4
St George's Place

Built in the high Victorian 'Byzantinesque' style of round arches and banded brickwork, this church has been deprived of its charm by a later balancing act (in 1914 by Jennings and Gray, who also designed the ill-proportioned 'Wren' church hall on the left) which added the matching right-hand turret and the central porch. The church is raised over a large school hall, and is interesting for its uncompromising emphasis on the central axis, derived from the old meeting houses. Organ, pulpit and baptistry, the latter lying under a mobile platform on which the communion table normally stands, are all on this axis, symbolising the central role of hymn-singing, preaching and adult baptism.

89
THE SIDNEY COOPER SCHOOL OF ART now COLLEGE OF ART
Founded 1868
St Peter's Street **Ionic portico c. 1870**

A typical example of Victorian paternalism, the College was founded by T. Sidney Cooper, a local boy who made good, and became one of the leading Royal Academicians of his day. Buying a handful of properties, he preserved his mother's house (the gabled front on the right), but converted the remainder to studios, and added, perhaps to his own designs, a pretty Corinthian vestibule (whose dilapidated condition today must be deplored), and an elonga-

▶ 88

ted and crisply detailed Ionic portico. Its charm goes undisputed today, and we need not take seriously, as indeed few people were doing by 1870, Pugin's comment: '. . . the eternal sameness of a Grecian temple outraged in all its proportions and character.'

90
AUCHER CLOSE 1869–70
41-6 London Road
Architect: J. G. Hall
Though somewhat aggressively picturesque, these six semi-detached 'Gothic' villas are pleasantly laid out round three sides of a small green, and provided at the time improved quarters for the six widows of the Aucher and Cogan Charity who had previously lived at Cogan's House (9). A proposed modernisation would remove the ornate leaded lights which form an essential ingredient, and are now almost unique in Canterbury.

91
GREENFIELD COTTAGES c. 1870
Off Gordon Road
Built as farmworkers' cottages, this rustic terrace has a factitious appearance of age deriving from the debased form of chequer work in flint and stone, which offers a pale echo of some fine mediæval buildings in the city [see St Mildreds' (29)]. The building materials were reputedly taken from the ruins of St Augustine's Abbey.

92
ROMAN CATHOLIC CHURCH OF
ST THOMAS BECKET 1874–5
Burgate
Architect: J. G. Hall
The forecourt was provided by the demolition of St Mary Magdalene, whose tower (30) remained standing, cramping the site and influencing the unusual north-south orientation. Erected literally in the shadow of the Cathedral,

it was opened in full pomp by Cardinal Manning. But its architecture is less glorious – an unorthodox assembly of Gothic parts in Kentish ragstone, with a central buttress-cum-turret-cum-bell-cote whose bizarre metamorphoses weaken so important a feature. The interior is a straightforward combination of nave, chancel and aisles with a rose window above the high altar. The new extensions by John C. Clague (1961–2) – a large chapel off the east aisle, and a hall above with separate access from Canterbury Lane – integrate admirably with church and street.

93
54 NEW DOVER ROAD   187

A considerable section of the New Dover Road including this property which is now a youth hostel, was a speculative development by a successful builder who later became mayor of the city. Details like the timber oriel or the superfluous-looking terracotta panels lack the self-assurance of the earlier houses across the road (84) and the result is a hotch-potch mitigated only by the picturesque effect of the tower.

THE CEMETERY CHAPELS 1876-7
Westgate Court Avenue
Architect: J. G. Hall

This is Canterbury's High Victorian monument,
and a compelling combination of classical planning and Gothic forms. It shows what the City
Surveyor could do when unhampered by site
restrictions. The central spire forms a triumphal
entrance, and provides side access to the two
flanking chapels, one of which (the noncon-
formist) is now disused. The carving, by Candy,
includes some ambitious gargoyles, and pro-
digious lace-like leaves for capitals and corbels.

95

**LONDON AND COUNTY BANK now
WESTMINSTER BANK** 1884-
The Parade
Architect: J. G. Hall

Hall's two banks [see also (98)], so near one an
other, are interesting to compare. Westminst
Bank is a well-proportioned palazzo-typ
street façade, exploiting to the full the effects
recession and projection. Superbly built
Kentish rag and Bath stone, its bizarre detail
like the suspended ædicules on the top floor, ar
not easily missed. In 1957 the Church of S
Andrew and the gate leading to it, which stoo

▶ 95

New Premises
High St Canterbury
for
Messrs. Pool and So

6 thick

tailed
9 in wall.

2 in projection

tailed
9 in wall.

tailed
9 in wall.

POOL AND SON

Section

Elevation

Scale ¼ inch = 1 foot.

Samuel Prentice
Surveyor

Lowell + Bro
Arch'ts
June 188

to the west, were demolished, and the gap was closed with a discreet extension by Dahl and Cadman.

96
POOL AND SON now ABBEY   **1887**
NATIONAL OFFICES
48 High Street
Architects: Cowell and Bromley
Built for a 'Military and Family Bootmaker' with a flat above, the building originally had two entrances on the ground floor, one for ladies and one for gents. Until 1900 the Church of St Mary Bredman stood next to it in what is now a small memorial garden. The façade of brick, stone and ornate terracotta panels, with its bold triple arch and quaint Ipswich oriel, is clearly influenced by the work of Eden Nesfield and Norman Shaw, though Cowell (who died at the age of 32) had in fact been a pupil of J. G. Hall, the City Surveyor. Ronald Ward and Partners, who turned the whole building into offices (1966–7), are responsible for the insensitive horizontal emphasis of rails in the triple arch.

97
21-3 NORMAN ROAD   **1887**
The character of this semi-detached villa, erected in Jubilee Year, is provided by the contrast of projecting bargeboards and bay windows with the recessed double doorway and medallioned niche above. The virtuosity of the pointed brick arches over window and door openings and the wealth of diapers, to name but two of several distinctive features, make this the quintessence of the better working-class dwelling.

98
MESSRS HAMMOND AND COMPANY
now LLOYDS BANK   **1888**
High Street
Architect: J. G. Hall
In contrast to Westminster Bank (95), Lloyds stands on the corner of two major streets, its red brick front broken by gables and oriels, and turning adroitly with a polygonal turret. Built in the early 16th-century secular style and based on Mr Hammond's own mansion at Nonington, its scale – two floors to the Abbey National's three next door – is somewhat inflated for the High Street. Hall died prematurely and before the building was complete. His other surviving works include the Presbyterian Church near the East Station, now threatened with demolition, and the amputated remains of the Congregational Church in Guildhall Street.

99
THE BEANEY INSTITUTE, ROYAL
MUSEUM AND FREE LIBRARY
High Street   **1897–9**
Architect: A. H. Campbell
This is the City Surveyor applying romantic gabling and florid half-timber work to a strictly symmetrical front, even to the point of repeating the quaint half-bow windows in the corners. The influence of Norman Shaw's domestic style was wearing thin by the end of the century, and here the already inflated scale becomes ludicrous in the carved brackets supporting the utilitarian-looking porch roof which was substituted for the embattled parapet of the original design. The new building – for a library and

museum which had been in existence since 1825 – became possible through the gift of Dr T. G. Beaney, a native of Canterbury who made his fortune in Australia. A later City Surveyor, H. M. Enderby, carried out internal alterations and substantial extensions at the back (1935).

100
THE OLD PALACE   **1897–9**
The Precincts
Architect: W. D. Caröe
The Archbishop's residence at Canterbury has been compared to a rambling country house squashed into the precincts of a cathedral. Its sprawling form incorporates remains of the old building, notably the 15th-century south wing

(with reception rooms) which provided Caröe with a style to follow. Archæologically important are the remains of the 13th-century great hall, traces of its south wall (including a polygonal stair turret) being built into the north wall of the new structure. The building as a whole is a highly competent welding together of old and new – three wings radiating from a central entrance hall, with the east wing turning a right-angle to provide a chapel. Caröe's manner, moreover, is rational enough; utilitarian in the west kitchen wing; ruthlessly archæological in the north wall (the jumble of windows and mediæval fragments is quite astonishing); faithful to the old in the restored south wing; and fanciful where he could be himself, as in the intricate porch details and chapel furnishings.

101
THE PAVILION   1900
St Lawrence Cricket Ground, Old Dover Road
Architect: W. J. Jennings
An elegant little timber-framed façade now
hemmed in by the large concrete stand (detached at least), and by a crudely abutting
extension on the right. The effect is achieved by
a clear distinction between structure (post and
lintel) and infill (shutters or just void), and by
the gentle axis of pediment, clock and Dutch
gablet.

102
POST OFFICE   1906–7
High Street
Architect: John Rutherford
Art nouveau seems to have missed Canterbury
except for a faint tinge discernible in this design
by one of the architects at the Office of Works.

As an essay in façade architecture it is one of the most skilful in the city, in scale with its surroundings, and equally striking in perspective from the High Street as in full frontal view from Best Lane. The eye is swept inwards along the elliptical hood moulds of the ground floor windows, guided upwards by the double oriel, and brought to rest on the deeply recessed gable window. Contemporaries were less enthusiastic. Sydney C. Cockerell, writing to *The Times* in 1907, drew attention to 'the poor and commonplace character of the Post Office buildings erected in various towns all over the country.'

103
LEFEVRE'S   1927
Guildhall Street
Architects: Jennings and Gray
The Theatre Royal designed by T. Sidney Cooper in 1861 was demolished to make way for these new premises for a family drapery firm, by the architects for the Baptist Hall (88) and other local buildings. The 3-storey steel-framed building is clad in white ceramic tile with period leaded lights to the upper floors. A major remodelling to the adjacent buildings was carried out at the same time, including the destruction of the fine classical façade to the Museum and Philosophical Institution at no. 14.

104
SIMON LANGTON GRAMMAR   1950
SCHOOL FOR GIRLS
Old Dover Road
Architect: Hugh Wilson, City Architect
This extensive complex was designed in 1948 as a three-form entry school at a cost of £209,000 to replace a school destroyed in the Second World War. The plan has a broad corridor system connecting one, two and three storey masses, and there is a separate dining hall and a gymnasium in addition to the assembly hall. The concept and construction clearly owe more to the prewar work of Gropius and Fry at Imprington College than to the rationalised systems for school building that were to follow five years later.

105
BURGATE HOUSE   1950
17–21 Burgate
Architect: J. L. Denman
A row of shops with separate residential accommodation over, one of the first permanent buildings erected after the bombing, and in a highly personalised neo-Georgian style, the brickwork and stone impeccably detailed. The eclecticism can perhaps be questioned in terms of its appropriateness to commercial needs in the second half of the 20th century, but the

104

105

arcaded pavilions, the small paned windows, and the broken roofscape certainly capture the right intimacy of scale and form within the context of the total street.

106
DAVID GRIEG SHOP   1953
St George's Street
Architects: Robert Paine and Partners

A large airy shopping space, the advertising advantages of the corner site being exploited to the full by the folded plate roof supported on cylindrical columns and wrapped round by a steel-framed screen clad in slate and glass; the contrast between structure and screen being particularly effective at night. The rear of the site is occupied by a more sober office and storage complex, although even here the roof structures echo those of the shop. The group was awarded an RIBA Bronze Medal in 1956. The exuberant use of slate, glass, steel, concrete, mosaic, travertine, and brick within one building date the design firmly. It shows the influence of the architecture of the 1951 Festival of Britain. Nevertheless it provides a welcome contrast to the architectural neutrality of the area of Canterbury rebuilt after the devastation of the Second World War. The pedestrian square created on the site of the Church of St George has great charm within which the David Grieg shop provides a fitting 20th-century complement to the sturdy remains of the tower (7).

107
WHITEHALL CLOSE HOUSING   1956
Whitehall Close
Architects: J. L. Berbiers, City Architect

On a site sloping down to the River Stour, and with easy pedestrian access to the town centre on one side and to open recreation space on the

other. This mixed development of maisonettes, houses and old people's bungalows forms a compact and socially well balanced group. Service and garaging areas are tucked behind the housing, and although the form of the maisonettes may appear dated, they fit happily with their neighbours.

108
LONGMARKET   1958–61
Architects: J. Seymour Harris and Partners
The Longmarket, running between St George's Street and Burgate, was badly damaged by enemy action in 1942, and the post-war plans, rather than rebuilding a covered structure, created an open pedestrian way with two-storey colonnaded shops built round an open square with a narrower finger leading towards the Cathedral. The architecture is reminiscent of the first-generation new towns, and the flat detailing is already affected by the weather. As

an urban environment the space is refreshing after the traffic of the main street, affording good views of the Cathedral over Burgate, and the interest of a change in level and organised floor-scape. Post-war rebuilding also provided the opportunity to carry out excavation, and amid the commercial bustle it is possible to see the remains of a Roman pavement. The major regret must be that this inward-looking scheme turns its back on to Butchery Lane, losing forever the sense of intimate enclosure and activity so admired in Mercery Lane, and such a feature of the pre-war Longmarket area.

109
TECHNICAL HIGH SCHOOL FOR GIRLS
Longport   1960
Architect: J. L. Berbiers, City Architect
This major extension to school premises in the

grounds of Barton Court (50) makes imaginative use of planting and the ornamental lake. The building is steel-framed on a 10-ft grid with brick and glass infill panels. The use of reinforced concrete floors allows the Assembly Hall to cantilever over the lake.

110
NASONS   1960
High Street
Architects: Robert Paine and Partners
An elegant widening of the High Street now leading to a furnishing store dates back to 1900

and the demolition of the Church of Saint Mary Bredman, (a 12th-century foundation rebuilt in 1828) and contains several interesting tombstones and a memorial to the men of the Royal East Kent Yeomanry. The entrance pavilion and showroom frontage built round a courtyard revert to the mediæval scale of the street, but the design is a brilliant contrast between the steel and glass cage with its timber pyramid-shaped roof and the traditional tile-hung gable of the main showroom. The pavilion leads to a spatially exciting interior by E. Gomme of High Wycombe with robustly detailed timber

framing and floors inside the original structure which is exposed in places revealing heavy timber lintels, brick arches, and even a sundial, lit now by perennially artificial suns. The external works and the pavilion received a Civic Trust Award in 1963, and the same architects are presently engaged in extending the showroom into the adjacent property.

111
UNION STREET REDEVELOPMENT
Union Street, Artillery Street area   **1961–3**
Architects: J. L. Berbiers, City Architect
A re-worked version of the 4-storey maisonette blocks, this time with opposed mono-pitch roofs, creates a major rhythm interspersed with 2-storey housing and a community building, across a site cleared of late 19th-century terraces. There are 200 dwellings in all, over half old people's housing, well situated next to a shopping street and 10 minutes walk from the centre of the city.

112
RICEMAN'S OF CANTERBURY   **1962**
St George's Lane
Architects: Sir John Burnet, Tait, Wilson and Partners
The replanning of the Whitefriars and St George's Street opened up an area previously notable for its tight, mediæval layout, and the effect has been to build along traffic arteries and to lose this essentially compact scale. In parts

the balance has been redressed by the provision of pedestrian squares [Longmarket (108)] but in this building the problem is compounded by the sheer bulk; five storeys of red brick, the length and width emphasised by the long horizontal bands of narrow windows. The roof terrace makes a fine vantage point and the canopied pavement-level windows do much to enliven an undistinguished bus terminus, but the presence of so assertive a building is clearly influential on other proposals for this area of the city.

113
CHRIST CHURCH COLLEGE   **1962–4**
North Holmes Road
Architects: Robert Matthew, Johnson-Marshall and·Partners
On land originally part of St Augustine's Abbey and enclosed on the street side by a substantial wall this College of Education for the training of teachers, an Anglican foundation, is built round a series of courtyards generally open on one side but with a central cloister-like area complete with colonnade and pool. The yellow brick buildings have a strong horizontal emphasis, heightened by white timber fascias and bands of windows. The courtyard planning makes for an intimate scale to the internal spaces, while the separation of the 7-storey student residential blocks at the south end of the complex avoids any conflict with the aluminium and glass roof of the chapel, axial to the main entrance, and containing a most interesting tapestry screen, which adds strong colour to this focal space.

78

112

113a

113b

114

115

114
29–33 WATLING STREET 1964
Architect: Anthony Mauduit

An object lesson in street infill. The centre block is a reworked version of an earlier re-building, the porch unifying two central doors, and lacks the sparkle of the flanking blocks. No. 29 is particularly successful at resolving the change in street line while keeping the character of the street, and it received a Civic Trust Award in 1966.

115
SESSIONS HOUSE Opened July 19
Longport

Architect: E. T. Ashley-Smith, County Archite
Adjoining the Sessions House (64), the ne section contains a court room together with t usual ancillary accommodation within tw stone-faced rectilinear blocks, the upper flo partly cantilevered and the whole seated on brick podium. The interior arrangements a well ordered and the approach up the main sta into the spacious entrance hall has an air dignity. The building tends to be swamped

the grand scale of the earlier work.

116

ELIOT COLLEGE
Designed 1963, completed September 1965

University of Kent at Canterbury
Architects: William Holford and Partners
Eliot was the first college of the University of
Kent at Canterbury which was founded in 1962
on an extensive site at the top of St Thomas's
Hill about 1 mile north-west of the city. The
view of the University from the town is of a
series of individual fortresses, as yet unleavened
by any serious attempts at integrating landscape,
although the trees of the adjoining woods and
round Beverley Farm have been retained and
well used. The long range view of the College,
and of Rutherford College, its mirror image
completed the following year, is of a defensive
wall, accentuated by slit windows which, while
preserving a sense of privacy within, add to the
monumental quality of the external appearance.
That the buildings appear self-contained is no
accident, since the college membership of about
600, half of whom are resident, is intended to
regard the College as a place for formal lectures,
seminars, reading, working, eating and relaxing
as well as a place to sleep. The complexity of the
function within a tight form turns the cruciform
plan into something of a maze, although spatially
the 3-storey hall and the brick cloister leading to
it achieve a satisfying scale and emotion, while
planned along a formal visual axis focused on
the Cathedral in the valley. The proliferation of
roof-top plant rooms suggests that the envelope
was too small for the contents, probably an
unfortunate consequence of the urgency of the
building programme.

117

PHYSICAL SCIENCES BUILDING
Completed September 1965

University of Kent at Canterbury
Architects: William Holford and Partners
The first teaching building on the University
site and adjacent to Eliot (116) and Rutherford
Colleges. Although designed at the same time,
the solution of the functional requirements has
produced a less monumental building than the
colleges. The horizontal separation of the heavy

workshops and vertical circulation from t[?]
sensitive operations of the laboratories produc[?]
an exciting architectural effect. The vertical se[?]
aration of the inward looking research a[?]
teaching laboratories on the first floor from t[?]
more open office and seminar rooms on t[?]
ground floor is also expressed in the elevation[?]
The two levels are linked by a steeply rak[?]
lecture theatre central to the main block.

118

BOILER HOUSE
19[?]

University of Kent at Canterbury
Architects: William Holford and Partners
A brick structure with twin metal flues, partia[?]
hidden in a grove of trees. The brickwork flow[?]
with great curved ends, round the enclos[?]
plant and the circular oil tanks like a miniatu[?]
castle, complete with surrounding earthwork[?]
Once within the private courtyard, the solidi[?]
of the brickwork contrasts with some 'fashio[?]
able' patent glazing.

119

POLICE HQ
19[?]

Upper Bridge Street, Old Dover Road
Architect: E. T. Ashley-Smith, County Archit[?]
Designed in 1963 as part of a group whi[?]
includes the Fire Station on the opposite si[?]
of the Old Dover Road, the building houses t[?]
District and Divisional Police HQ. A group[?]
crisply articulated blocks, the horizontal natu[?]
of the offices is emphasised by the separation[?]
the frame from the brick and glass cladding, t[?]
whole achieving considerable success in the u[?]
of materials. The dark brick and the flint-fac[?]
cladding panels harmonise well with the ci[?]
wall, and contrive at the same time to appe[?]
business-like without losing the right urban a[?]
yet human scale.

120

43 IVY LANE
19[?]

Architects: Dudley Marsh, Son and Partner[?]
Well scaled street infill on a restricted site ne[?]
to the best surviving Wealden house in Cante[?]
bury (25), this 2-bedroomed house is notab[?]
for its use of double-height living space and t[?]
open tread staircase enclosed in a brick ha[?]
drum.

► 119

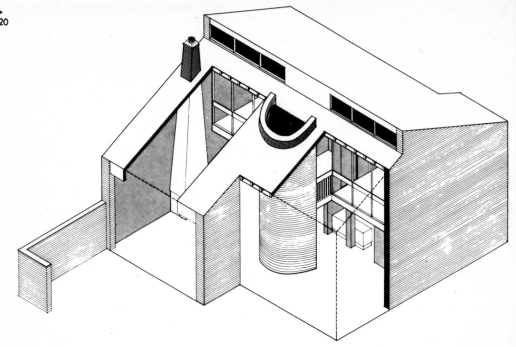

► 121a

► 121b

121

THE OLD RECTORY, 1966
OFFICE DEVELOPMENT

37 Old Dover Road

Architect: Anthony Mauduit

A speculative office development built round a
Grade II listed building. The use of unequal
bands of grey-white brick interspersed by
painted timber windows, double glazed and
incorporating sun blinds, makes an elegant
exercise in proportion. The same brick is used
internally with arched forms and concrete, and
gives a sense of completeness to the design.
Excellent use of existing garden trees round the
site and in the car park area.

122

UNIVERSITY LIBRARY

Phase 1 completed 1967

University of Kent at Canterbury

Architects: William Holford and Partners

Planned as the first of four phases, the completed section has a capacity of 200,000 volumes and houses basic administration; reader spaces are restricted since the colleges provide study areas. Externally the building is an essay in the articulation of form and materials; the interior is technically efficient, the scale and finish of the major spaces tend towards the theatrical.

123
TECHNICAL HIGH SCHOOL FOR BOYS
Spring Lane   1967
Architects: J. L. Berbiers, succeeded by D. H. Tomkinson, City Architect
A three-form entry school, steel-framed on a 10-ft module; the solid infill panels here are an insulated sandwich with a white porcelain enamel finish, the movement between the frame, glass and panel being covered by an aluminium bead. The lightness of this construction contrasts well with the dark brick of the traditionally

built service block. The entrance to the school is effective, the massing being arranged to produce a natural yet exciting focus. Being on an open site, this building makes an interesting comparison with the immediate post-war school (104) and clearly shows the effect of technological advance and tight cost control.

124
NEW CLASSROOM BUILDING   1967
King's School
Architects: Robert Paine and Partners
A 2-storey brick addition to an existing classroom building and a rare example of modern design within the Precincts. The windows have deep reveals with raked brick spandrel panels; the whole composition having a sculptural permanence, in character with the surroundings.

125

ROBERT BRETT AND SONS, OFFICES AND VEHICLE MAINTENANCE BUILDING 1967

Wincheap

Architect: John C. Clague

A straightforward concrete-framed building with brick infill and metal windows; the column spacing derives from the width required for two gravel tipper trucks. The strength and simplicity of the whole design capture the right functional quality.

126

ACCIDENT CENTRE 1967

Kent and Canterbury Hospital

Architects: George, Trew and Dunn

A large 2-storey structure in concrete and brick housing the first phase of a major expansion of the hospital. The building is planned round a series of light courts, the ground floor containing the Accident Centre and various temporary departments, with two wards and operating suites on the first floor. The form of the plan necessarily makes for lengthy travel, but the generous width of the circulation routes gives the building an open quality.

127

HALES PLACE HOUSING 1967–70

Architects: J. L. Berbiers, succeeded by D. H. Tomkinson, City Architect

Hales Place estate was given by Elizabeth I to the Manwood family in 1563 (33) and until 1926 the house was used as a Jesuit seminary. The entire 35 acres are now being developed by the city as the latest 'out-town' housing community. The first 40 units completed in 1967 used dark brick and flat roofs; the second phase of 270 units are in a lighter brick, with horizontal cladding panels and shallow pitched roofs. The terraces are generally ranged along the contours of the steeply sloping site giving dramatic views

over the city. The detailing to the brick steps and retaining walls is good. Shops and community buildings are proposed, and will help to create a cohesive social climate.

128

EXAMINATION AND SPORTS HALL

University of Kent at Canterbury 1968

Architects: Williamson, Faulkner-Brown and Partners

A totally introverted building, generally accepted as being one of the finest sports halls in Europe. A major block, consisting of a playing floor some 36 metres square with 2-storey changing, lounge and administration areas under the same roof, is linked by a fully glazed entrance hall to a smaller block containing four squash courts. The form of the building, inside and out, stems directly from the satisfaction of the precise functional needs for heat, light, sound, safety, and playing surface. It has aptly been described as 'a big box surrounding a good floor'.

129

KEYNES COLLEGE Completed 1968

University of Kent at Canterbury

Architect: William Henderson of Farmer and Dark

Designed to a modified brief and on a more limited budget than the first two colleges, the form here reverts to the more traditional collegiate plan, open quadrangles and a greater separation of social and private rooms. The building is notable for the crisp concrete and blockwork detailing; the change to a textured

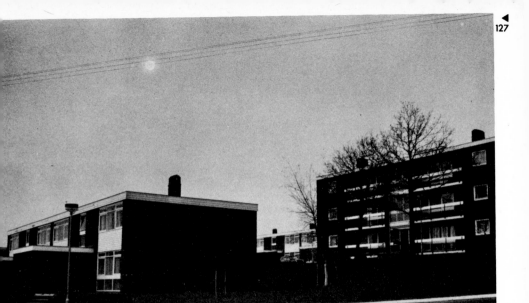

block for the stair towers gives an emphasis to their counterpoint in the overall window pattern. The use of stained timber internally tends to cheapen the effect, but the building has a real sense of humanity. The site is treated sympathetically, trees and water being used to full advantage. The Master's house guards the well-detailed entrance road like a toll booth, contriving to retain its own identity while firmly part of the College.

130
GULBENKIAN THEATRE 1969
University of Kent at Canterbury
Architect: William Henderson of Farmer and Dark
A 6-sided auditorium with seating for 350 arranged round three sides of a stage which has moderately variable geometry. The rich wall and furnishing colours and the good acoustics assure the audience of a proper sense of occasion, but access to the stage is very limited and hardly makes up for the technical sophistication of the equipment.

131
SWIMMING POOL 1970
Kingsmead Road
Architects: Robert Paine and Partners
Part of a recreational zone, already containing a sports stadium and youth centre, being developed by the City of Canterbury to serve a regional catchment area. The basic design was completed in 1964 but the economic climate delayed construction for five years. The main elements of the design are a 33.3 metre pool and a separate learners' pool within a simple concrete framed enclosure, boldly detailed in rib finished concrete and copper faced felt. From the swimmer's view its delight will be in the use made of the south-west orientation. A glazed wall to the main pool overlooks a screened sun-bathing court which is to contain gymnastic equipment, and at a higher level a roof terrace over the changing and locker facilities has views back into the pool. Provision is made for spectators in raked seating internally, with tinted glass and deep mullions used to reduce glare.

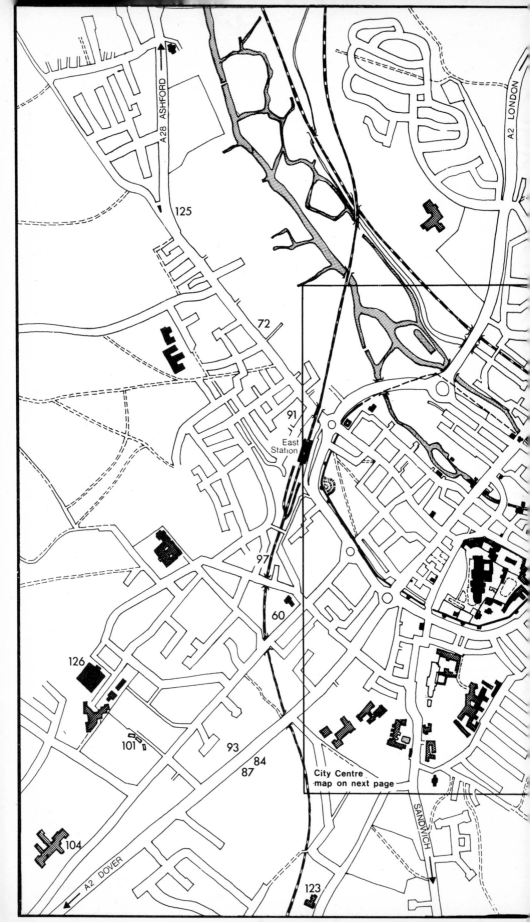

A 28 ASHFORD

A 2 LONDON

125

72

91

East
Station

97

60

126

101

93

84

87

City Centre
map on next page

SANDWICH

104

A 2 DOVER

123

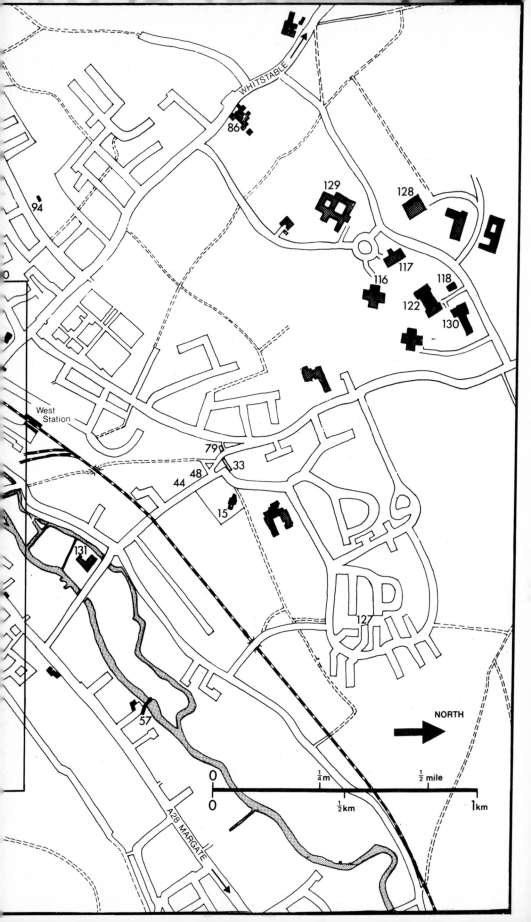

WHITSTABLE

94

86

129

128

117

116

118

122

130

West
Station

79

33

48

44

15

131

57

127

NORTH

0   ¼ m   ½ mile

0   ½ km   1 km

A28 MARGATE

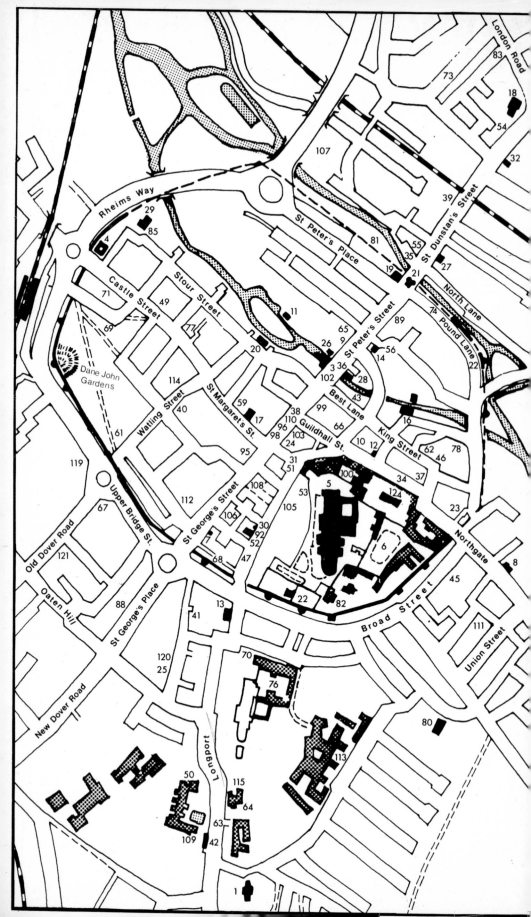

INDEX

Entries in *italic* are to textual reference only to prominent architects and planners and not to any specific example of their work.